The Philosophy & Foundations of Vocational Education

The First Volume in MSS' Series on Vocational Education

Papers by
H. C. Kazanas, James N. Harris, C. Dale Lemons et al.

MSS Information Corporation
655 Madison Avenue, New York, N.Y. 10021

Library of Congress Cataloging in Publication Data
Main entry under title:

The philosophy and foundations of vocational education.

    1. Vocational education--Philosophy--Addresses,
essays, lectures. I. Kazanas, H. C.
LC1042.5.P45   370.11'3   73-10249
ISBN 0-8422-7124-4

11/2/79 Berhart Tyler 17.00

TABLE OF CONTENTS

CREDITS AND ACKNOWLEDGEMENTS

Barlow, Melvin L., "Vocational Education as a Social Movement," *American Vocational Journal*, 1969, 44:30-32.

Bensen, M. James, "The Function and Structure of Industrial Arts in the Educational Philosophy of Alfred North Whitehead," *Journal of Industrial Teacher Education*, 1967, 5:5-13.

Brown, Bill Wesley, "Industrial Arts — An Educational Responsibility for Interpreting Technology," *Man/Society/Technology*, 1972, 32: 47-53.

Burkett, Lowell A., "Vocational Education at the Crossroads," *American Vocational Journal*, 1968, 43:13-15.

Coe, Burr D., "What is Quality Vocational Education?," *American Vocational Journal*, 1968, 43:16-17.

Crawford, Lucy C., "Basic Beliefs in Distributive Education," *American Vocational Journal*, 1968, 43:24-26.

Glazener, Everett R., "Foundations of Industrial Education," *Journal of Industrial Teacher Education*, 1970, 7:5-8.

Hansson, Kenneth S., "Industrial Educators in Sweden: Their Status and Their Education," *Journal of Industrial Teacher Education*, 1968, 5:52-65.

Harris, James N., "Objectives and Standards of Industrial Technology," *Journal of Industrial Teacher Education*, 1970, 8:17-23.

Kazanas, H.C., "A Model for Reorganizing the Comprehensive High School," *Journal of Industrial Teacher Education*, 1972, 9:11-21.

Kazanas, H.C.; and L.C. Wolff, "Development of Work Habits in Vocational Education — What the Literature Indicates," *Journal of Industrial Teacher Education*, 1972, 10:48-58.

Koble, Ronald L., "Foundations of Industrial Arts Education," *Journal of Industrial Teacher Education*, 1970, 7:18-20.

Kuntz, Elmer, "The Use of Census Data for the Implementation of Vocational-Technical Education Programs," *Journal of Industrial Teacher Education*, 1972, 10:32-37.

Larson, Milton E., "The Philosophy Education Forgot," *American Vocational Journal*, 1968, 43:22-23.

Lemons, C. Dale, "The Man Society Technology Forum," *Man/Society/Technology*, 1972, 32:3-8.

Maley, Donald, "Relationship of Industrial Arts to Occupational Orientation," *Man/Society/Technology*, 1972, 31:209-213.

Maley, Donald, "The Responsibility of Industrial Arts for Interpreting Technology," *Man/Society/Technology*, 1972, 32:58-62.

Pautler, Albert J., "A Conceptual Curriculum for Industrial Arts and Occupational Education," *Industrial Arts and Vocational Education*, 1968, 57:26, 36, 76, 78.

Stadt, Ronald W., "Industry Aids Education," *Journal of Industrial Teacher Education*, 1971, 8:28-31.

Task Force on Vocational-Technical Education, "Changing the Context in which Occupational Education Takes Place," *American Vocational Journal*, 1968, 43:59-60.

Warmbrod, J. Robert, "New Designs in Vocational and Practical Arts Education," *American Vocational Journal*, 1967, 42:53-58.

Wirth, Arthur G., "John Dewey vs. the Social Efficiency Philosophers," *Man/Society/Technology*, 1972, 31:170-172.

PREFACE

The proper role of vocational education is to provide a bridge between man and his work. Occupation sets the tone of social relationships, influencing as it does the standard of living, the solidarity of the family, and the quantity and quality of civic participation and responsibility. Especially in a technologically fluid society, it becomes imperative for men and women to have available a permanent, universal, and continuing program of vocational education, one which teaches basic concepts like good work habits, and which provides job-related upgrading and retraining to match the pace of technology. Therefore it is clear that a sound educational base is essential for success in all types of jobs. Vocational counselors and instructors are vitally concerned in the development of inclusive and viable programs.

MSS' introductory volume in a new series on vocational education surveys recent literature on the philosophy and foundations of this relatively new field. Opening papers deal with the objectives of vocational education departments in high schools, current standards of technological and industrial education, and models for comprehensive reorganization of the present system. Particular emphasis is placed on the question of the quality of vocational education programs as they now exist throughout the country.

Albert Pautler
September, 1973

Philosophy

DEVELOPMENT OF WORK HABITS IN VOCATIONAL EDUCATION—WHAT THE LITERATURE INDICATES

by

H. C. Kazanas and L. C. Wolff

INTRODUCTION

The main purposes of vocational and technical education are to help the individual develop desirable and effective work habits and acquire the necessary knowledge and skills of an occupation to either enter and/or make progress in it. Through the years, however, vocational educators have concentrated their efforts in teaching and developing skill performance competencies and treated the area of effective work habits as an incidental factor in their vocational programs. One explanation for treating the area of effective work habits as an incidental factor has been the feeling that work habits are taught and learned along with the psychomotor skills or "caught in the process of education". This may be true in some occupations but in general, effective work habits have not been included or emphasized in many vocational courses of study as an integral part of the curriculum. Furthermore, most vocational educators would agree that as technology is advancing, the area of effective work habits becomes more critical because many of the skills once performed by the worker are now performed by machines. Thus, the worker finds himself in a work-environment where desirable work attitudes and effective work habits become the criteria for survival on the job. In other words, effective work habits are becoming increasingly important, and vocational educators preparing youth for employment should take special notice of this fact. The purpose of this paper is to review the research on work habits relating to vocational and technical education and present some implications for program improvement purposes.

RELATIONSHIP OF THE WORKER, WORK HABITS, AND THE JOB

The term "work habits" is susceptible to review in more than one context, a restricted or a broad context may be suggested. In the restricted context, an individual is in fact engaged in a specific, limited work activity. In this context, it can be stated that a work habit is a constant pattern of action, an unconscious process by which the work is performed. In this case, the term applies to a work activity that is so well established that it occurs almost without conscious or

10

explicit thought on the part of the worker. Inferred in this situation is a "conditioned response" to a work activity and therefore, repetition may be instrumental in the acquisition of this type of work habits.

In a broader context, numerous responsibilities described as "work habits" are associated with an individual's daily life and are part of his daily work. The term is not restricted to a particular work activity, neither can it be restricted to operations, tasks or duties performed on the job by an individual. Other aspects require consideration. In the popular sense, work habits encompass a number of generally accepted responsibilities such as reporting for work each day, being on time, obeying orders, practicing safety, not loafing on the job and so forth. This suggests that there may be two kinds of work habits. Those which are general in nature and may be found to be present in most types of occupations and those which are specific in nature and are characteristic of a specific occupation or a cluster of closely related occupations.

In discussing work habits, work attitudes are also involved. Therefore, to clearly understand work habits, an understanding of work attitudes is essential. Unlike the lack of a clear definition of work habits, work attitudes may be defined as the manner in which an individual views his work, or as a state of mind or a feeling with regard to his work. This indicates that there is a close relationship between work habits and work attitudes. It appears that while monetary rewards and prestige may be strong motivations to work, positive attitudes toward work are the most basic foundations of effective work habits. A positive attitude toward work is a great American tradition rooted in the protestant ethic of our work oriented society. This may suggest that to maximize training on effective work habits, positive attitudes toward work may be a necessity. Ideally then, for an individual to be productive in his work, he must have a positive attitude toward his work and have learned effective work habits and skills of the occupation of his choice.

Thorne, Boles and O'Leary (1950) suggested that effective work habits are learned by intensive training according to the psychology of learning. They state that:

> The ability to work efficiently is a function of a complexity of factors which appear to be learned rather than instinctive or intuitive. In the higher species of animals showing working behavior, it usually is necessary to provide intensive training in the desired patterns to "break" the animal into proper work habits. Experiences in "breaking" horses, training hunting or working dogs, oxen, etc., indicate that animals in the "wild" state may survive very well when left to their own resources but become progressively more untrainable and resistive to regulation with increasing age as their own habitual reactions become established. Even in the "working" species known to be susceptible to training (hunting dogs), animals which fail to be trained early in life and are allowed to roam uncontrolled soon become "outlaws" and become refractory to all further training attempts.

11

Analogous behavior is seen in human "wild" children and adults who have never learned good work habits. Persons who become vagabonds as children or whose early circumstances made work unnecessary, find it very difficult to exert the self-control necessary to develop good work habits later in life (92-93).

Work habits like attitudes, are learned and formed at an early time in life (Hoyt, *et al.*) and deeply engraved and persist throughout life and at very old age they may even compensate for the decline of certain mental activities of the individual.

The study of work habits in vocational and technical education should be directed toward a critical examination of how individuals acquire effective work habits by identifying and analyzing work habits to determine those work habits which are desirable for selected occupations and or occupational clusters. In addition, procedures should be identified and selected which the vocational teacher may employ to teach and develop such effective work habits in his vocational students assisting them to become more productive on the job and happier in their chosen occupation. The proper place to start developing effective work habits is the home. Hoyt, *et al,* (1972) state that "the home, as a work place, constitutes a viable laboratory for teaching basic concepts of work to children (112)."

STATUS OF RESEARCH ON WORK HABITS

It is interesting to note that the literature and research dealing with work habits is filled with subjective material and the majority of the studies can be categorized as normative and descriptive in nature rather than experimental. On the other hand, many experimental studies have concentrated in the area of psychomotor skill acquisition in psychology and education. No research studies dealing with work habits have been identified in vocational and technical education. Furthermore, while a great deal of research has been done by industrial engineering researchers in the area of human performance, no studies have been conducted specifically in the area of work habits. Perhaps this group of researchers assumed that efficient production methods, processes and movements repeatedly done for a given operation or task will result in developing work habits in the worker for that particular task. This may be true for certain types of jobs but it seems that the high absenteeism and dissatisfaction with highly repetitive tasks may suggest that attention should be directed to study the area of work habits in the broad context as defined earlier in this paper.

Although the subject of work habits is as old as work itself, studies dealing with this area did not appear until the modern psychology of learning was supplied. And even then, work habits have been studied in numerous settings by individuals characterized by different interests, specialties, and backgrounds rather than psychologists and vocational educators. It is of interest to note that educators were not involved in the study of work habits until the federal government commenced sponsoring specific job related programs. The results of their undertaking have culminated in the accumulation of some data which is inconsistent and so diverse that it makes categorization of studies and generalization of results a difficult task. The categories which follow seem to offer a logical means for review of the literature and research completed on work habits.

RELATIONSHIP OF WORK HABITS
AND PERSONALITY ADJUSTMENT

Thorne, Boles and O'Leary (1950) observed that there is a relationship between work habits and personality adjustment and that work habits are an essential foundation to mental health. Manifestations of this relationship are found in the increased emphasis placed by modern psychiatry on occupational therapy as a means to improve mental health of certain mental disorders. On the other hand, poor work habits may serve as etiologic causes or symptoms for personality maladjustment. To explore the relationship of work habits and personality adjustment, Thorne, Boles and O'Leary organized and conducted an educational workshop. Sixteen factors which may contribute to work habits were identified and analyzed. For each factor, a psychological analysis, a set of measurement methods and suggested remediation methods were also identified. The 16 factors identified were seriousness of purpose, industry, initiative, perseverance, concentration, responsibility, influence, concern for others, self-criticism, emotional stability in work, budgeting time, following directions, seeking advice, use of research sources, organization of materials and accuracy. It appears that all of these factors are work habits of the broad context suggested earlier and therefore are common factors which may apply to any occupation rather than to only specific occupations. In conclusion, Thorne, Boles and O'Leary state that:

> Good work habits contribute more dependably to happiness and personality growth than any other activity in which a person may indulge . . . . The objective, then, is not to seek a life of leisure but of creativeness; not to find relaxation in idleness; but in a change of work; not to seek happiness in old age in retirement from work but to keep busy as long as life lasts (100).

WORK HABITS AND THE MENTALLY RETARDED

In recent years, an interest in the mentally retarded youth and adults has generated several studies in the area of work habits for these type of individuals. Folsom (1966) conducted a study with secondary school educable mentally retarded youth. Two aids were developed by the researcher, a four-point rating scale consisting of 12 specific work habits and a workbook with five daily lessons on each of the 12 work habits. The purpose of the study was to ascertain whether the use of these two aids with the 12 selected work habits would bring about improvements on work habits of the mentally retarded. The work habits used in the study were: being on time, using time wisely, finishing a job, having initiative, getting along with others, enjoying work, being neat, following directions, doing satisfactory work, following safety rules, taking care of equipment and working independently. It was concluded that although some improvement was evident, the results were influenced significantly by the teacher or by other intervening variables rather than the method used.

In a parallel study, Neuhause (1967) attempted, during a research demonstration project, to teach educable mentally retarded adults typical job skills which would result in selected good work habits. He concluded that although job skills may be acquired by this type of individual, it does not automatically assure success in the development of personal skills and adequate work habits. The most important factor was not teaching the mentally retarded job skills but assisting them to develop adequate and mature personal social skills—effective work habits.

WORK HABITS AND ACHIEVEMENT

Several researchers have attempted to establish a relationship between work habits and achievement at different levels of education. O'Leary (1955) used four standard tests and two researcher-made instruments with ninth grade students. The purpose was to identify the relationship of work habits to over- and under-achievers. The Work Habits Rating Scale (WHRS), consisting of 15 selected work habits, was developed and validated to rate the identified work habits. Most of the 15 work habits used in the scale were the same identifed by Thorne, Boles and O'Leary (1950). Those habits were: industry, concentration, seeking advice, following instructions, responsibility, budgeting time, organization of materials, research skills, starting and finishing tasks, seriousness of purpose, initiative, use of factual materials, self-evaluation, influence on others and emotional reactions. Using a multiple correlation technique, it was found that a relatively high correlation existed between work habits, achievement, mental age and study skills. O'Leary concluded that the WHRS is a useful scale in predicting whether or not students will work to or beyond their capacity and that the scale appears to be a reliable and valid instrument for that purpose.

WORK HABITS AND THE THEORY OF "INDUSTRIOUSNESS"

In a series of research studies, Krathwohl (1949a, 1949b, 1951a, 1951b

14

and 1953), attempted to set forth a "Theory of Industriousness". He developed a scale—the Index of Industriousness (I.I.) which provides a measure of industriousness on work habits enabling an individual to achieve over his ability level as revealed by an aptitude test in any particular field. Krathwohl's I.I., which constitutes the backbone of his theory of industriousness, is important and based on the idea that for a given degree of an individual's brightness as measured by his aptitude scores, the harder the individual works or the higher his scores on the I.I. scale, the greater will be his achievement. Krathwohl's Index of Industriousness, for mathematics for example, is the difference of a student's derived score on the mathematics aptitude test. More specifically, Krathwohl (1949a) stated that:

The hypothesis on which industry or indolence was established in college mathematical work was that if grades were a function of ability and not of habits of industry or indolence, then the average college algebra grades for the industrious, normal and indolent groups should be the same for the same ability. Instead of that, it was found, without exception, that the average grades of the industrious students in college algebra always were higher than those of the normal group of the same brightness; and the average grades of the indolent group, without exception, always were lower than those of the normal group of the same brightness (366).

Krathwohl contends that the greatest advantage of the theory of industriousness is the ease with which a counselor may secure information concerning the work habits of students from their test scores and use those scores as predictors of success in the various subjects.

Krathwohl's theory of industriousness has been criticized by Juola (1953). In his analysis of Krathwohl's theory of industriousness, he has concluded that:

The Index of Industriousness is an interesting and perhaps illuminiating way of measuring the influence of a student's work habits, but its relationship to class grades in English cannot be considered higher than going by the correlation coefficient of .06. Since the relationships to other subjects were not given, they cannot be any higher. Considering the relationship of the I.I. to later class grades for only specific aptitude levels is meaningless. The I.I., when this is done, loses its meaningfulness and is reverted back to the original achievement test scores with the aptitude held constant. A theory of work habits which is based upon the I.I., seems to have a very weak foundation indeed, since the only condition under which the I.I. can be considered useable lies in reverting the scores back to the measures from which they were obtained (311).

15

WORK HABITS AND DESIRABLE PERSONAL
AND SOCIAL TRAITS

Bruner, (1932), Brody, (1952) and Green, (1958), have attempted to establish a relationship of work habits and personal and social traits. Bruner reviewed characteristic traits of selected subjects by analyzing the performance of two types of movements designed to represent typical work habits. The results indicated that the tasks performed generated distinguishable changed in emotions of the subjects, but their characteristic traits did not vary significantly. On the other hand, Brody directed his attention to a group of college women to ascertain developmental factors which may affect work habits and selected social traits. The instruments used were records of aptitude tests, questionnaires and peer judgments.

It was concluded that women dormitory residents, who are well integrated, capable, responsible and highly motivated, are also those who have good work habits. Green, in an opinion article, directed her attention to the development of personal traits and work habits through clerical office practice. She was concerned with the idea of whether work habits are "taught" or "caught" in the educational process. She identified and analyzed such desirable work habits and personal qualities that can be (and should be) taught in the classroom as the ability to attack problems successfully, the ability to handle directions, the ability to utilize time and materials efficiently, the ability to work independently, a wholesome attitude toward work, a pleasing personal manner, poise and self-assurance and concern for detail and accuracy. She concluded that the ability to get along with others is one of the most needed qualities of any worker and that it involves both good personality traits and good work habits.

METHODS OF TEACHING WORK HABITS

Delfosse (1956), dealt with the problem relative to the methods of teaching work habits. Although several methods have been suggested and used, no simple method seems to have been isolated that was found superior to all others. In a study using films to teach work habits, Delfosse found that motion pictures are useful in presenting effective work habits. He concluded that a review of films may help persons acquire less fatiguing work habits and that repeated showings of the films may help to eliminate wasted motion, regulate time and shorten work cycles.

In recent years, the federal government has emphasized the need for developing effective work habits. As a result, several programs, Rull and Moore (1968), U.S. Office of Education (1968), and the U.S. Department of Labor (1965, 1968), have focused on work habits in terms of practicality and essentiality in the world of work. The U.S. Department of Labor (1965) provides a handbook prepared expressly for young men who are working in

16

service stations. The handbook contains general information and summarized safe work habits in performing the job normally assigned to service station attendants. In a similar effort, Rull and Moore (1968), initiated a phase of a demonstration program designed to provide dropout prone students with an opportunity to obtain pre-employment experiences and training. This program provided the participants with the opportunity to develop not only skills but also effective work habits and positive attitudes. Furthermore, both the U.S. Department of Labor and the U.S. Office of Education have prepared workbooks which emphasize the need for developing effective work habits for disadvantaged individuals in the automotive trades.

SUMMARY

Research indicates that the acquisition of work habits cannot be taken for granted. It has been stated that work habits are not instinctive, they are learned through training in accordance with the psychology of learning. The pre-school child leans work habits in the home. Parents, therefore, should be aware of this fact and meticulously guide and encourage the child to learn good work habits through demonstrations, patience, praise and time. The normal child is inquisitive and invariably has a strong drive to copy the actions of parents or his immediate associates. It has been suggested that parents performing work in the home, take the time to teach the child various meaningful tasks that may lead to effective work habits. Simple tasks are first to be learned, followed by progressively difficult ones. Selectiveness is essential to match difficulty with maturity, and avoid child frustration. Interest retention is also essential. Helping the child learn effective work habits is important for his latter development in school.

After the child enters into the primary grades, he (or she) is exposed to a new environment, new situations and new routines. Work habits such as arriving on time, obeying rules, departing for home at a certain hour, must all be systematically emphasized and learned. The teacher's role in guiding pupils as they learn new work habits is a formidable one at the primary grades. The expression "a place for everything and everything in its place" seems relevant in helping children acquire work habits. Classroom arrangement, routines, encouragement, allowance for individual differences, clear instructions, realism and praise are included in the list of teaching techniques that may be used to assist students to learn good work habits.

It has been stated that work habits learned effectively are not easily forgotten or thrown out of an individual's inventory. A person with "shoddy" work habits may have a difficult time in adjusting to a job requiring many new work habits, especially if he has to unlearn certain "bad" work habits before he starts learning good ones. Old established work habits offer resistance and tend to override new ones that may be essential. This suggests a concentrated effort to avoid ineffective work habits. A person with ineffective work habits will likely experience difficulty in replacing them with effective work habits. This may result in dismissal from the job.

Work habits have been found to be a critical factor for the mentally retarded and the disadvantaged. For these individuals, it is not enough that they be taught skills to compete in the job market, but also it is equally important that they acquire effective work habits to obtain gainful employment. Given basic work skills and effective work habits, there is little reason to expect that the educable mentally retarded and the disadvantaged cannot be useful workers in our society. In an effort to achieve this objective, a new emphasis has been placed in recent years in job related programs designed to help the disadvantaged and handicapped obtain employment in meaningful jobs. These programs sponsored by the federal government, provide, among other features, handbooks with general information on certain jobs but the unique characteristic of these handbooks is the inclusion of suggestions on human relations and effective work habits.

Briefly stated, the approaches to the study and acquisition of effective work habits are numerous and varied. Also, work habits have been found to be related to many factors. Work habits are influenced by fatigue, feeblemindedness, methods of operation and movements. Work habits have been related to achievement, personal and social characteristics and traits, work efficiency, industriousness and personality adjustment.

In the past, vocational educators have concentrated their efforts in developing in their students, effective psychomotor skill performance. In general, the area of work habits has been treated as an incidental factor and usually dealt with in a haphazard manner. It is evident that as technology progresses, more psychomotor skills are performed by machines and the worker finds himself in a work environment where effective work habits become the criteria for survival on the job. It is important, therefore, that the vocational teacher take cognizance of work habits as an important adjunct to psychomotor skill development and assign appropriate priority to the tasks of teaching and developing effective work habits in his vocational students. Occupational development is not complete until both occupational skills and effective work habits have been learned effectively.

Work habits can be identified for any occupation or occupational clusters. They can be analyzed and broken down into specific elements for instructional purposes. However, the methods by which work habits can be identified and broken down into specific elements for instructional purposes have not been adequately researched. Therefore, a great need for research on work habits is present. The research completed thus far has not dealt with effective work habits of specific occupations or occupational clusters. The identification of work habits and the processes of teaching and acquiring them are areas that vocational educators must direct more concentrated research effort.

18

REFERENCES

Brody, D.S., *Developmental factors affecting sociality traits and work habits among college women.* Unpublished doctoral dissertation, University of Minnesota, 1952.

Bruner, W., *A comparison of measurements on a movement apparatus and typical work habits.* Zurick: Leemann, 1932.

Delfosse, M.G., Use of films in study of work habits. *Travail Humaim,* 1956, 19, 51-77.

Folsom, G.S., *An assessment of a program for the development of work habits for educable mentally retarded youth at the secondary level (with) good work habits: A workbook designed for use in dissertations.* Unpublished doctoral dissertation, University of Alabama, 1966.

Green, H.H., Development of personal traits and work habits through clerical office practice. *Business Education Forum,* 1958, 12, 17-19.

Hoyt, K.B., et al. *Career Education,* Salt Lake City: Olympus Publishing Company, 1972.

Juola, A.E., A criticism of studies utilizing the 'Index of Industriousness' as a measure of work habits. *The Journal of Educational Research,* 1953, 47, 307-311.

Krathwohl, W.C., The persistence in college of industrious and indolent work habits. *The Journal of Educational Research,* 1949, 42, 365-370.

Krathwohl, W.C., Effects of industriousness and indolent work habits on grade prediction in college mathematics. *The Journal of Educational Research,* 1949, 43, 32-40. (a)

Krathwohl, W.C., Relative contributions of vocabulary and an index of industriousness for English to achievement in English. *The Journal of Educational Psychology,* 1951, 42, 97-104. (b)

Krathwohl, W.C., A theory of work habits of industriousness, *Journal of Engineering Education,* 1951, 42, 157-163. (c)

Krathwohl, W.C., Relative contributions of aptitude and work habits to achievement in college mathematics. *The Journal of Educational Psychology,* 1953, 44, 140-148. (d)

Milwaukee Vocational, Technical and Adult Schools, Wisconsin, United States Department of Health, Education and Welfare, Office of Education, Division of Manpower Development and Training, Washington, D.C., *You and your job: What is it? Where is it? How to get it. How to keep it. Where do you go from here?* Chicago: J.G. Ferguson Publishing Company, 1968.

Neuhause, E.C., Training the mentally retarded for competitive employment. *Exceptional Children,* 1967, 33, 625-628.

O'Leary, M.J., *The measurement and evaluation of the work habits of over-achievers and under-achievers-to determine the relationship of these habits to achievement.* Unpublished doctoral dissertation, Boston University, 1955.

Rehabilitation Research Foundation, Elmore, Alabama, United States Department of Labor, Washington, D.C., and United States Department of Health, Education and Welfare, Washington, D.C., *Work habits in the automotive trades,* 1968.

Rull, M.H. and Moore, R.O., A demonstration training program for potential school dropouts. *A service station training school for dropout-prone students.* Quincy Public School District 172, Illinois, Southern Illinois University, Edwardsville and United States Department of Health, Education and Welfare, Office of Education, Washington, D.C., 1968.

Thorne, F.C., Boles, L.S., and O'Leary, M.J., The relation of work habits to personality adjustment. *Journal of Clinical Psychology,* 1950, 6, 91-101.

United States Department of Labor, Bureau of Labor Standards, Washington, D.C.; *Service station safety for young workers,* 1965.

OBJECTIVES AND STANDARDS OF INDUSTRIAL TECHNOLOGY

By James N. Harris

Industrial Technology curricula have been initiated in colleges and universities throughout the United States in direct response to the needs of industry. As a result of the accelerated activity leaders in industrial technology education have become more responsive to the necessity of appropriate objectives and standards that may be used for establishing and or evaluating four-year industrial technology programs. Educational representatives are also becoming more cognizant of program quality (outcomes) as an important factor in appraising the increasing demands for paraprofessional personnel who can function effectively in the coordinating and management functions of industry.

Until recently, there was no organized leadership to deal with problems associated with evaluative standards for industrial technology education. This situation is reflected in reports now being furnished by agencies and organizations as they examine the technology education movement. The National Association of Industrial Technology (NAIT), as well as other groups have assumed major responsibility for bringing about the establishment of industrial technology education guidelines. In addition, the National Science Foundation (NSF) is supporting an important study, currently underway, to determine, among other factors, the status and focus of engineering and industrial technology education and perhaps to suggest directions.

FORMULATING PROGRAM OBJECTIVES

Prior to establishing specific program objectives for industrial technology curricula, it is first necessary to set up broad goals and general purposes of the program that reflect the philosophical values held by all persons concerned—students, faculty, administration and community leaders—with respect to the desired outcomes of the educational experience. Once the broad goals of the program have been established, specific program objectives which are consistent with the aims of the educational institution need to be formulated.

Brackenburg (1967) stated that "objectives are to the educational enterprise what destinations are to a ship—both teaching and seamanship require direction if they are to have meaning and significance (p. 89)." An objective has been described as a description of an intended change in the performance of students—a statement of what the performance level of the student is supposed to be when he has completed prescribed educational experiences or after he has been exposed to certain definable activities in the on and off-campus environments. In contrast with purposes, objectives are more explicit statements descriptive of the competencies which a program purports to develop in students (Dressel, 1963, p. 21). A statement of an objective includes:(1) an identification of the intended educational accomplishments; (2) a detailed operational definition involving observable and measurable competencies; and (3) the establishment of standards or criteria of what are considered acceptable behavioral changes in the light of consistent, meaningful, and workable philosophy for the educational institution.

One problem in formulating objectives is that educators have often failed to

21

recognize that there are various levels of objectives and that objectives at each level differ from those of another in specificity and origin. The three levels of objectives are societal, institutional, and instructional. Objectives at one level cannot effectively serve at another level until they have been reformulated. Therefore, to be effectively implemented, objectives must first be reformulated in order to be useful for the level at which they must serve. Effective instruction and learning in industrial technology education, therefore, is highly dependent upon closely related and thoughtfully formulated objectives.

Specific program objectives usually need to meet the following criteria: (1) exhibit relevance to the basic philosophy of the educational institution; (2) show compatibility with students' acceptance and desire to learn; (3) show realistic correspondence to what can be effectively taught in terms of available physical facilities, staff qualifications, library resources and fiscal capability; and (4) facilitate interaction of student and instructor by providing the basis for a continuous two-way feedback that will serve to motivate and direct effective teaching and learning (Biedenbach, 1970, p. 1).

THE NEED FOR STANDARDS AND GUIDELINES

The current interest in standards and guidelines for four-year industrial technology programs is best reflected in the recent report, "Standards and Guidelines for the Accreditation of Baccalaureate Industrial Technology Programs" (NAIT, 1970). A careful study was conducted over many months to derive, what are considered, acceptable and educationally sound standards for accrediting industrial technology programs. A basic assumption of NAIT is that achievement of prescribed evaluative standards enhances the professional standing of industrial technology programs. Industrial technology curricula with the following purposes have been endorsed by NAIT:

1. Those combining liberal education with professional-level technical emphasis. These would be in the industrial fields including design, production, communication, transportation, and power.
2. Programs which include general education with appropriate mathematics and science.
3. Those programs which prepare students for leadership responsibilities in industrial planning, supply, product utilization and evaluation, production supervision, management, market research and technical sales.
4. Those programs which reinforce industrial production, management, and marketing with appropriate laboratory experiences.

NAIT has also established the following evaluative standards for industrial technology programs relative to curricula, instruction, students and related services:

Curricula

Department, Division, and School Goals. The purposes of the academic unit and its major administrative structure, as an initial point of reference, should be compatible with the national objectives of Industrial Technology.

Curricular Emphasis and Characteristics. Primary emphasis of the curriculum should reflect the technology of contemporary industry. A reasonable balance between the practical application or "how" and the conceptual emphasis of "why" should be in evidence. This curriculum should in turn lead to the baccalaureate degree.

22

Course requirements for the baccalaureate degree should be defined in each area of specialization, specific concentration or option within Industrial Technology offered. Options may be rather varied and bear such titles as Quality Control, Industrial Design, Manufacturing Technology, Production Management. Certain options may reflect greater degrees of specialization such as Electronics or Metals Technology. Whatever the curriculum, it should be relevant to the required job competencies as indicated by industrial employers.

Curriculum development, reassignment and evaluation should involve those responsible for the instruction. It should include not less than the junior and senior years of baccalaureate study and appropriate lower division requirements, either in the same program or in articulation agreements which have been developed with other institutions such as the community colleges.

Interdisciplinary Relationships. The interdisciplinary relationships of various courses, such as math and physics with mechanical systems, should be evident. The curriculum should be flexible and quickly reflect new changes within industry and the "state of the art."

The curricular "mix" should be compatible with the following minimum percentages of foundation-type course offerings. This curricular foundation should be supplemented by the institution being evaluated or by the individual students with additional or different course offerings.

TABLE I

MINIMUM-MAXIMUM FOUNDATION PERCENTAGES OF 4-YEAR BACCALAUREATE PROGRAMS OF NOT LESS THAN 120 SEMESTER UNITS

Area of concentration	Percent
General Education — Humanities, English, History, Sociology, Psychology, Speech, Economics and Similar fields	15-30%
Mathematics — Trigonometry, Analytical Geometry, Calculus, Statistics	10-20%
Physical Sciences — Physics, Chemistry	10-30%
Management — Production Control, Quality Control, Manufacturing Cost Analysis, Engineering, Economics, Supervision, Production Management, Plant Layout, Time and Motion Study, Personnel Management, Accounting, Business Law, Marketing, etc.	10-20%
Technical — Plastics, Metalworking, Foundry, Welding, Electronics, Drafting, Mechanical Systems, etc.	20-30%
Electives	5-15%

Instruction

Instructional Methods Utilized and Emphasized. The emphasis in the instructional program should relate directly to the stated local objectives and goals. Of major importance are practical industrial type applications. Laboratory work has a realistic and pertinent role in the instructional process. Methods used should be those which effectively motivate students.

Faculty Qualification. Faculty qualifications should include emphasis upon:

(a) Extent, recency and pertinence of academic preparation, (b) Extent, recency and pertinence of industrial professional-level experience (such as supervision-management), (c) Extent, recency and pertinence of industrial non-professional level experience (such as the technician work,) and (d) The procedures used in the selection of faculty that result in maintaining and improving the quality of instruction.

Tenure and Retention Policies. Tenure and retention policies should include incentives for professional improvement, salary and fringe benefits comparable to the national averages, and recognition of additional academic preparation. Also to be weighed are industrial experience, teaching experience and the quality of teaching.

Faculty Loads. Teaching loads should be determined and assigned on a basis that promotes quality instruction. Policies and procedures used in the assignment of advisees to faculty contribute to effective counseling. The faculty's assigned professional responsibilities other than teaching and advising should be consistent with a quality program in Industrial Technology.

Quality of Instruction. Effective motivation of students should be evident. The organization and scheduling of instruction should be effective. Effective use should be made of suitable instructional aids.

Faculty Professional Contributions. There should be evidence of effective faculty efforts related to such professional matters as consulting work, attendance at professional society meetings, research and publications.

Students

Admission Standards and the Counseling of Students. New students should be required to meet certain minimum standards such as graduation from high school or an Associate Degree from a community college or a technical institute. Adequate services should exist for the counseling of new and continuing students.

Sources of Students and the Recruitment of Students. Sources of students and recruitment procedures should be such as to assure the selection of students capable of graduating and achieving success in industrial employment related to the program.

Scholastic Success of Students. Industrial Technology students should have scholastic success comparable to those in other curricula in the institution and to industrial technology programs nation-wide. The grading procedures in Industrial Technology courses should be comparable to those of other departments in the institution.

Success of Graduates. The initial placement, job titles, job description and salary of graduates should reflect achievement of the program's stated objectives. Emphasis is placed upon follow-up studies of graduates. These studies should be conducted on a regularly scheduled time basis, possibly every 2-3 years, with accurate records maintained. Included should be reports of promotion of graduates to positions of greater responsibility. The percentage of graduates going on to graduate school and their success in graduate school is significant. Industry's reaction to the graduates as employees must be favorable. An evaluation of the baccalaureate industrial program should be made by its graduates. Their reactions and recommendations should be considered for future improvement of the program.

Enrollment Trends in the Program. The program should have a record of growth since it was started. This growth should compare favorable to state, area, and national industrial technology growth rates. Enrollment growth factors affecting the past, present, and future should have been identified. Future enrollment projections, with justifications, should have been prepared.

Related Services

Physical Plant Facilities and Equipment. The facilities and equipment should be adequate to meet instructional and related needs of the present and the immediate future. Long-range plans should have been made for the future of the program. The facilities and equipment should be adaptable to new developments in industry.

Finances. Finances should be adequate to provide the necessary faculty, facilities, equipment, support personnel, supplies and other needed aids.

Library and Related Services. Both the quality and quantity of library and audio-visual resources should provide strong support for the instructional program.

Industrial Relationships. Industry Advisory Committees, or similar direct consultation and support should be utilized. Students should have first hand contact with industrial personnel, procedures and manufacturing processes. This could include resources speakers, field trips, and co-op work-study programs.

Placement Services. These services should include both related summer jobs and permanent jobs and should be available to industrial technology students. The placement office should initiate services to students beyond perfunctory referrals.

EVALUATIVE CRITERIA

There are a number of factors which may influence the effectiveness of industrial technology programs in terms of prescribed standards. This effectiveness is based, in large measure, on the success of the program in achieving the goals for which it was organized. The program is usually judged by its own results (outcomes) rather than by comparison with some other program.

A major purpose for developing program standards is to establish bases by which evaluative procedures may be carried out and to assist persons responsible to make objective judgments about validity of the curricula. Program standards should provide guidance for establishing new programs, facilitate student transfers, and provide information about qualified graduates for prospective employers.

Evaluative standards that have been designed for engineering type programs are not entirely suitable for industrial technology curricula because of the heavy design and mathematics orientation. While there may be some areas of similarity between given programs, there are major differences in objectives and curricula content (general education), which distinguishes engineering based programs from those in industrial technology.

TOWARD AN INDUSTRY-COLLEGE DIALOG ON CURRICULA

The job title of "technologist" in industry is a relatively new designation in a majority of United States companies. Although many persons with job titles of engineer are in reality currently performing duties which the Bachelor of Science in Technology graduate is capable of doing, industry has been slow in recognizing this change in the over-all collegiate or university technology curriculum. It is rapidly becoming apparent, however, that many engineering job classifications, especially the manufacturing and production oriented industries, can be handled more effectively by technologists who are in general more device-oriented and who are interested in working with people and solving practical everyday industrial problems.

Many engineering graduates from colleges and universities today are highly oriented in basic science and mathematics and are not strongly motivated to work on the level required to solve many of the problems facing industry today. In addition, many top level two-year technicians currently on industry payrolls are being encouraged to upgrade themselves to the technologist level. Many highly qualified engineers, in order to justify the salaries they now receive, are being asked to increase their productivity by concurrently assuming the directorship of several related projects and allowing the technologist to put the overall plans for any one of the projects in operation with the help of technicians.

In general, the computer has become the basic tool used by engineering groups to simulate many of the design problems that currently must be solved to make available to the general public devices and solutions to many technical and social problems. The technologist, as an integral part of this engineering team effort, will become more and more involved in the details of these simulations in the foreseeable future. Regardless to the type technologist being considered, he must understand the fundamentals of computer science to work effectively with his engineer-supervisor. Some industries have begun to recognize this need, and as a result, are developing extensive in-house technology programs to educate employees who are motivated in this area of training.

SUMMARY

It has been emphasized that certain salient features characterize any strong industrial technology program. These features must be based on worthwhile objectives and must be effectively implemented. Objectives must be based on clearly identified educational needs and implementation requires an effective thoroughly informed organization equipped with well defined procedures.

Standards and guidelines that include suggested objectives have been developed by NAIT for evaluating industrial technology curricula in direct response to the steadily increasing number of requests made by educational institutions.

One observer recently summarized some of the current thinking about the technology education movement as follows: (1) with the wide range of technology programs around the country, the job of drawing up a common denominator and clear definitions are indicated; (2) engineering and technology are not clear terms; they mean different things to different people; (3) the National Commission on Accrediting (NCA) is demanding better clarification on standards being used for the accreditation of technology programs; and (4) more Deans need to know what is going on in their programs.

Finally, two important factors necessary for the growth and development of viable industrial technology programs are students seriously dedicated to the proposition of learning and competent faculty currently involved in "state-of-the-art" technology education. The personnel responsible for the operation of industrial technology programs, including the students, are critical components in the health and well-being of any progressive industrial technology program. It is important that all feedback channels for program evaluation remain open. Effective student participation in the evaluation of program objectives and standards should be given careful consideration. To be of value, however, the feedback information should be assessed and appropriate conclusions must be drawn and acted upon.

REFERENCES

Biedenbach, Joseph M. Computer courses in an industrial continuing education program for technologists. Paper presented to the American Society for Engineering Eucation, Columbus, Ohio, June 24, 1970.

Brackenbury, Robert L. Guidelines to help schools formulate and validate objectives. **Rational planning in curriculum and instruction**. Washington, D. C.: National Education Association, 1967.

Dressel, Paul L. **The undergraduate curriculum in higher education.** Washington, D. C.: The Center for Applied Research in Education, 1963.

Harris, James N. **Proposed criteria for self-evaluation of four-year industrial technology programs.** (Doctoral dissertation, The Wayne State University) Detroit, Mich.: 1969.

Krathwohl, David R.; Bloom, Benjamin S. & Masia, Bertram B. **Taxonomy of educational objectives. New York: David McKay, 1964.**

Michael, William B. and Metfessel, Newton S. A paradigm for developing valid measurable objectives in the evaluation of educational programs in colleges and universities **Educational and Psychological Measurement,** 1967, 27, 373-383.

Moss, Jerome. Evaluation of occupational education programs. Technical Report of the Research Coordination Unit in Occupational Education, the University of Minnesota, September, 1968.

The National Association of Industrial Technology, Standards for accreditation. **Report to the national commission on accrediting.** Washington, D. C.: 1970.

A MODEL FOR REORGANIZING THE COMPREHENSIVE HIGH SCHOOL

by
H.C. Kazanas

During the last decade the social, economic and technological changes in our society have had an unprecedented effect on vocational-technical education. As a result of these changes, a dramatic shift in the emphasis on vocational education has occurred in the United States. The shift has been both quantitative and qualitative in nature; quantitative in terms of more vocational education for more youth than ever before and qualitative in terms of making vocational education relevant to the needs of youth and society. The shifting of emphasis toward vocational education has culminated in several legislative measures which are revolutionizing the field. Since 1964 the quantitative dimension of vocational education has resulted in a steady increase in vocational education enrollment at all levels. This increase has been from 349,000 in 1964 to an estimated 8.1 million in 1968 and is projected to be about 14 million by 1975 (Russo, 1969).

Although vocational-technical education has made great strides in the past decade, ''the failure of our schools to educate to the level of adequate employability nearly 25% of the young men and women who turn 18 each year is a waste of money, as well as of human resources'' (National Advisory Council on Vocational Education, 1969). Marland (1971) pointed out that:

> Of those students currently in high school, only 30 percent will go on to academic college-level work. One-third of those will drop out before earning a baccalaureate degree. That means 80 percent of the present high school students should be getting occupational training of some sort. But, only about a quarter of these students are getting such training. Consequently, half our high school students, a total of approximately 1,500,000 a year are being offered what amounts to irrelevant general educational pap! (28).

In other words, these youth need some form of occupational education at the high school level to make the transition from high school to employment and/or from high school to higher levels of occupational preparation.

The role of providing a ''bridge'' for the transition from high school to employment is (or should be) as important in our society as the traditional role of providing a ''bridge'' for the transition from high school to college. Though it is as important to provide education for the vocationally oriented youth as it is to provide it for the college oriented, providing education for college oriented youth still remains the *primary* purpose and effort of the secondary school. All to frequently it appears that the purpose for providing education for college oriented youth is the responsibility of the *entire* faculty of the high school, while the purpose of providing education for vocationally oriented youth is assumed to be the responsibility of only a few so called "vocational teachers." Frequently, teachers of academic subjects, and many times even the principal and his assistant principals, are not involved in planning and organizing meaningful experiences relative to the present and future employment needs of non-college bound high school youth who represent about 80 per cent of the students in the school. As Marland (1971) put it "there is illogic here as well as massive injustice (28)."

In recent years many attempts have been made in terms of more money, new programs, renovated physical facilities; to mention only a few, with the purpose of improving vocational education. However, limited effort has been directed toward improving the administrative structure of the comprehensive high school and thus improve the over-all effectiveness of this institution where more than 66 per cent of vocational education is offered (AVA, 1971).

This paper is an attempt to: (1) analyze the basis of organization of the comprehensive high school; (2) propose a model for reorganizing the comprehensive high school and (3) relate this model to vocational education in the comprehensive high school.

BASIS OF ORGANIZATION OF THE COMPREHENSIVE HIGH SCHOOL

Recent statistics indicate that approximately 66 per cent of all vocationally oriented students are enrolled in the comprehensive high schools (AVA, 1971). This makes the comprehensive high school the most important institution for providing occupational education at the secondary level. However, an analysis of the administrative structure of the comprehensive high school would indicate that this institution was originally organized on the same basis of organization as the traditional secondary school or even as the early American academy. But there is good reason to believe that the major purpose and function of today's comprehensive high school is somewhat different from that of the traditional high school or early academy. The major purpose and function of the traditional high school has been to prepare students for college, while the major purpose of today's comprehensive high school should be to help students achieve their vocational, avocational and subsequent educational goals (Michael, 1958; Wenrich, 1957, Conant, 1959). This suggests then that the comprehensive high school must be a multi-purpose institution in order to meet the needs of youth and society (Conant, 1959, 1961). Inasmuch as administrative form should follow the functions of the organization, this institution would then require an administrative structure that could support its functions. Such an organization should be different from the traditional form of organization found in most high schools today.

Furthermore, it has been suggested by many theorists of organization that human activity may be organized into institutions of various types and sizes on the bases of (1) major *purposes* or *functions* served; (2) major *processes* used, (3) *persons* or *things* dealt with or served and (4) *place* or *location* where service or activity is rendered (Gulick, 1937; Marx, 1946; Pfiffner and Sherwood, 1961). However, in any institution the *major goals* to be achieved should be the main determinant of the basis of organization. Institutional success or failure will depend, to a great extent, on whether the basis of organization is in terms of the job to be done and/or the goals to be achieved (Skogsberg, 1955). This should not be taken to mean that all institutions must have a single base of organization. Obviously, a small, simple institution may use only one basis while a large institution may require more than one to function effectively. However, when an institution is organized with more than one basis of organization, one should predominate; otherwise there is an institutional fracture consistituting an unsurmountable obstacle to efficient operation and to needed institutional modifications. It has been suggested that the comprehensive high school is partly organized under a *purpose-based* organization, but predominately is organized under a *process-based* organization (French 1946, 1957).

A *process-based* comprehensive high school organization is one in which the instructional program and the faculty is organized under subject-matter departments, such as English, mathematics and social science, and these subject-matter departments exist and function merely to teach the particular subject matter involved without any coordinated effort to achieve a *major purpose* of the school. French (1945) stated that:

> In a comprehensive high school where the instructional program is organized into departments representing each teaching field (and in the area of foreign languages, for example, into even smaller departments) an average of about 60 percent of the time of pupils is spent in the study of academic subjects. This is a process organization of the work which experts in institutional organization agree usually results in an over-emphasis of the techniques involved in the various processes and an under-emphasis on the major purposes to be served by an institution (404-405).

Thus, *process-based* high school organization and subject-matter departmental organization are the same—they refer to the traditional form of organization (Figure 1). The subject-matter departmental organization was, to some extent, adopted by the early secondary school from the expanding business and industrial organizations during the late nineteenth and early twentieth centuries (Skogsberg, 1950). As such, it carried over with it the early practices and theories of organization developed by Taylor, Fayol, Urwick, Gratt, and other early management theorists. It was basically an organization based on production. It was structured into sub-groups each in the line of authority for the sole purpose of production, control, and efficiency— taking advantage of specialization. By sub-grouping and specialization, the process could be done with greater excellence, thus quality control and production efficiency were more easily established and maintained. As Cook (1960) pointed out such an organizational structure requires that:

All decisions on procedures and design are made at the top and passed down from authority level to authority level. In this order of production, departmentalization came into being. As a supervisory and directing authority, the department head laid out the work, directed the teaching, and checked the learning results by a standard measure of achievement. The organization worked well in industry. However, in education, the raw material with which the teacher worked was animate; it reacted to process and not always in the same pattern. It was this important difference in raw material which gave difficulty to the subject-centered curriculum, as children with every intellectual capacity entered the high school (121).

The subject-matter departmental organization was then adopted by (or carried over to) the comprehensive high school from the early American secondary school and it is still the predominant type of organization today. Through the years this type of organization has had its critics. The American Association of School Administrators (1958) stated that:

Although the organization of the faculty by subject field departments is traditional and although certain functions can be performed best through this means, the controlling consideration should be the most effective plan for accomplishing the ultimate purposes of the school. If departmentalization is the dominant basis of organization of the faculty, it may actually retard the realization of the ultimate purposes of the school. There is an increasing awareness of the conflict between strong faculty departmentalization and a balanced educational program (192).

Skogsberg (1954) summarized some of the criticisms raised against the subject-matter departmental school organization as follows:

The conventional basis of staff organization found in our secondary school conceives of education as a series of more or less unrelated processes. Subject teaching departments are prominent. Each one works on a vested interest idea in competition with others. The essential base of the organization is *process.* In practice, experience has shown that some of the results of this process-based organization are: (1) promotes a feeling of working in a sphere of a specialty in competition with other specialists; (2) engenders a feeling of teacher isolation with a subject matter area; (3) gives impetus to the idea that all students should be

31

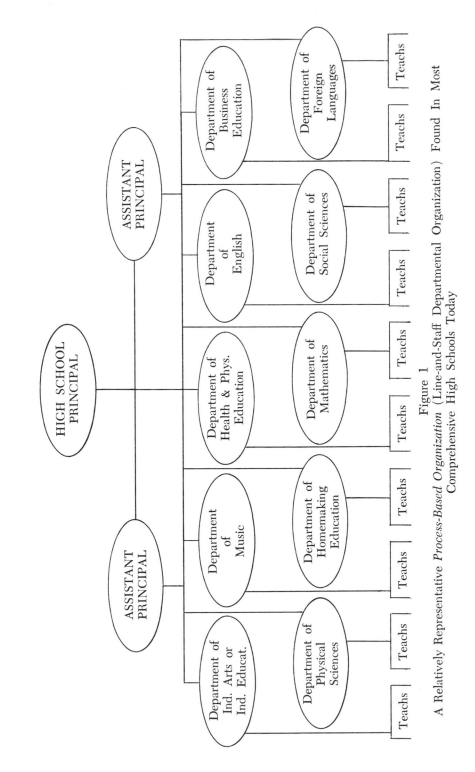

Figure 1

A Relatively Representative *Process-Based Organization* (Line-and-Staff Departmental Organization) Found In Most Comprehensive High Schools Today

required to take some departmental pet subject regardless of need or plan; (4) continues subjects in the curriculum long after they have lost their usefulness to pupils—classical Greek, for example; (5) confuses ends and means; (6) bolsters organizational rigidity to the point of inflexibility; (7) advances status differentiation beyond the usefulness in organization (275).

To meet the student's vocational, avocational and subsequent educational goals, the comprehensive high school must be a multi-purpose institution. Therefore, the most appropriate administrative structure should be one prompted by its *major purposes.* If the comprehensive high school emphasizes mastery of particular subject-matter techniques, it becomes chiefly concerned with processes. Thus, part of its major purposes cannot be effectively accomplished. Furthermore, its teachers and administrators "specialists" in a particular subject, would tend to view the learning process through accomplishment in their subject-matter and techniques rather than through the student's over-all development (Cook, 1960).

THE PURPOSE-BASED MODEL FOR REORGANIZING THE COMPREHENSIVE HIGH SCHOOL

An analysis of the *major goals of secondary education* developed by professional organizations would reveal that the high school in our society exists to achieve certain major purposes of secondary education (Educational Policies Commission, 1951, 1961; National Association of Secondary School Principals, 1951; French, 1957). Therefore, if the comprehensive high school is to be responsive to the needs of all students, it requires an administrative structure that permits each student to achieve his vocational, avocational, and subsequent educational goals. Such an organization must be based on the major purposes of secondary education. In other words, the comprehensive high school must be purpose organized rather than process organized (French, 1946, 1957; Skogsberg, 1955; Cook, 1960).

Some of the suggested major purposes of secondary education that could serve as the bases of high school organization are *citizenship education, home and family living education, health education* and *career education* (French, 1957; Education Policies Commission, 1961; National Association of Secondary School Principals, 1951). For the comprehensive high school to meet its goals effectively, it should be organized under these (or other) major purposes of secondary education. However, although several major purposes of secondary education have been developed and could be used for high school organization, they have not been universally accepted by the educational community. Some educators argue that the present day high school should have only two major "purposes"—to prepare the student for college or for immediate employment upon graduation (Marland, 1971). It appears,

therefore, that for the comprehensive high school to be *purpose-organized* the major purposes of secondary education must be defined. Once the major purposes of secondary education are defined, then the organization of the high school can be structured based on those major purposes.

The proposed model of a *purpose-based* comprehensive high school organization requires that for each of the major purposes defined in the school, an administrator should be responsible for deploying the available resources for achieving that major purpose in the school (Figure 2). The administrators of all major purposes, the high school principal and representative citizens of the community would constitute the executive committee of the high school responsible for the over-all planning of the school curriculum. On the other hand, the administrators responsible for each major purpose of the school would be responsible for achieving that major purpose by helping every teacher

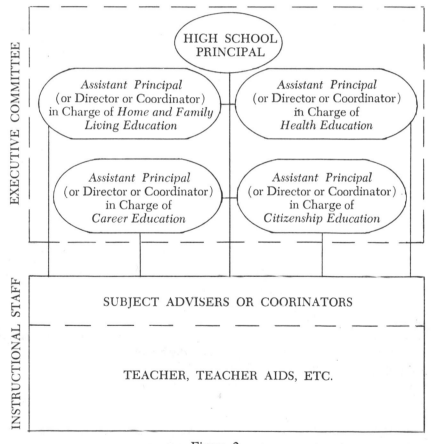

Figure 2
One Way The Comprehensive High School May Be
Organized Under A *Purpose-Based* Organization

34

obtain the educational outcomes desired in each subject in relation to the objectives of the major purpose involved and the over-all purposes of the school. When such administrators (assistant principals, supervisors, directors, coordinators, or whatever the title) are employed for each of the major purposes they would tend to be ''generalists'' of a major purpose rather than ''specialists'' of a specific subject in the curriculum. Thus, they would not necessarily have preferences in subject-matter offerings other than the contribution a particular subject can make to the achievement of one or more of the major purposes of the comprehensive high school.

Some of the possible advantages that may be found in a *purpose-based* school organization are: (1) promotes intrafaculty unity in terms of the total education of the student; (2) focuses the faculty's attention on the student and his needs, rather than on some predetermined artificial hurdle such as the acquisition of a particular body of knowledge or subject; (3) achieves better faculty integration and feeling of teamwork in the total school effort; (4) provides more attention to what kind of students are turned out; (5) utilizes more the total potential of the faculty through committee involvement; (6) is more flexible, more adaptable, and taps much more of the leadership ability of the entire faculty; (7) minimizes status differentiation among faculty members due to strict subject-matter affiliation; (8) provides for better integration of the educational process (Skogsberg, 1961).

VOCATIONAL EDUCATION IN THE PURPOSE-BASED COMPREHENSIVE HIGH SCHOOL ORGANIZATION

In the traditional *process-based* (departmental) high school organization, vocational education is conceived of as a number of unrelated occupational service areas organized into independent departments each responsible for providing occupational experiences related to specific skills in an occupation or occupational area. This type of departmental organization may be effective in providing certain highly specialized occupational skills, but it is relatively ineffective in providing for the over-all development of the student. As a result one of the major purposes of the comprehensive high school—career education—is not fully achieved.

To achieve the over-all development of the vocationally oriented student, he is often sent to other subject-matter departments to acquire competencies in related subjects such as mathematics and science. However, in many cases these subject-matter departments are college oriented departments and their subject-matter has been designed and organized to meet the needs of the college oriented student. Therefore, the occupationally oriented student finds himself in courses which are irrelevant and unrelated to his needs and goals. To assist the student in his over-all development, the *purpose-based* high school organization appears to be one of the ways for providing an *integrated program* within the general area of lifework (career) education of the school.

Furthermore, due to the present *process-based* school organization, most vocational teachers (and sometimes vocational administrators) tend to isolate themselves from the rest of the faculty and administration of the school. Thus, basic decisions affecting vocational education in the school are made by faculty and administrators who have limited knowledge of and preparation in vocational education and who are mostly "preoccupied with college-entrance expectations (Marland, 1971; p. 27)." Therefore, to alleviate the massive injustice done to about 80 per cent of the high school students, as Marland pointed out, the high school organization must be reorganized from a *process-based* to a *purpose-based* organization.

In the *purpose-based* school organization, an administrator (Figure 2) would be responsible for achieving the major purpose of career education of the school. However, in order for the administrators responsible for that major purpose of the school to function effectively, they must be trained in, among other things, a comprehensive vocational education program. These administrators should not be vocational service area oriented, as most of the present day vocational administrators are, but rather they should view occupational education in terms of the contributions it can make in assisting each student in the school to achieve his goals.

As with most proposed models, the model for reorganizing the comprehensive high school proposed in this paper has not been tested and its effectiveness or ineffectiveness is not known. However, with the present rate of investment toward improving and expending vocational (career) education as well as the entire secondary education, testing of this model is not only possible but highly desirable. An experimental program can be established and a number of comprehensive high schools can be selected to participate. Their present *process-based* organization can be reorganized to a *purpose-based* organization for an experimental period of at least four years. The faculty of those schools can be prepared on an in-service bases to function effectively under the *purpose-based* organization. The financial support needed for this experimental program may come from the U.S. Office of Education under the allocation for career education since the reorganization of the comprehensive high school into a *purpose-based* organization will not only affect vocational education but the entire educational process in secondary education and hopefully will make career education more effective.

SUMMARY

Though approximately 66 per cent of the vocationally oriented students are presently enrolled in the comprehensive high school, most efforts to improve vocational education have been made outside the comprehensive high school. Such efforts as area vocational schools, skill centers, Junior College vocational programs, to name only a few, have had definite impact on vocational education. However, the comprehensive high school still remains a relatively untapped source for improving occupational (career) education. This is because we were led to believe that the comprehensive high school is effective in providing vocational education. However, statistics cited herein indicate that this is no longer true. It appears that much effort needs to be directed toward improving occupational education in the comprehensive high school. One way of doing this is by improving the comprehensive high school's administrative structure to make it more responsive to the vocational, avocational and subsequent educational goals of the vocationally oriented students.

The proposed *purpose-based* school organization may be considered as one of the ways for improving the administrative structure of the comprehensive high school. It may well be that investment by the federal government in an experimental program in reorganizing the administrative structure of the comprehensive high school toward the *purpose-based* organization proposed in this paper will prove to be a most worthwhile venture in American secondary education.

REFERENCES

American Association of School Administrators. *The high school in a changing world.* The Thirty-six Yearbook, Washington, D.C.: AASA, 1958.

American Vocational Association. A profile of vocational education. *Member-Gram,* 1971, 2 (4).

Conant, J.B. *The American high school today.* New York: McGraw-Hill, 1961.

Cook, B.J. *A study of the department head in the comprehensive high school.* Unpublished doctoral dissertation, Rutgers University, 1960.

Educational Policies Commission. *Education for all American youth: A further look.* Washington, D.C.: National Education Association, 1951.

Educational Policies Commission. *The central purpose of American education.* Washington, D.C.: National Education Association, 1961.

French, W. The postwar high school should be purpose-organized, *Teachers College Record,* 1945, 46, 404-405.

French, W., et al. *American high school administration policy and practice.* New York: Rinehart, 1957.

Gulick, L. Notes on the theory of organization. *Papers on the science of administration.* New York: Columbia University, Institute of Public Administration, 1937.

Marland, S.P. Career education now. *School Shop,* May 1971, 30, 27-28, 43.

Marx, F.M. *Elements of public administration.* Englewood Cliffs, N.J.: Prentice-Hall, 1946.

Michael, L.J. Innovations in the organization of the high school. *The high school in a new era.* Chicago: The University of Chicago Press, 1958.

National Advisory Council on Vocational Education. *Annual Report.* Office of Education, U.S. Department of Health, Education, and Welfare, 1969.

National Association of Secondary School Principals. *Planning for American youth.* Washington, D.C.: National Education Association, 1951.

National Committee on Secondary Education. *Education for work.* Washington, D.C.: National Association of Secondary School Principals, 1967.

Pfiffner, J.M. and F.P. Sherwood. *Administrative organization.* Englewood Cliffs, N.J.: Prentice-Hall, 1961.

Skogsberg, A.N. Basing staff organization on purpose. *Phi Delta Kappan,* 1955, 34, 213-218.

Skogsberg, A.N. *Administrative organizational patterns.* New York Bureau of Publications, Teachers College, Columbia University, 1950.

Pusso, M. 14 million vocational students by 1975, *American Education.* Washington, D.C.: U.S. Office of Education, 1969.

Venn, Grant. Vocational education for all. *The Bulletin of the National Association of Secondary School Principals.* 1967, 51, 32-40.

Wenrich, Ralph C. Can the comprehensive high school fulfill its promise? *School of Education Bulletin.* Ann Arbor, Michigan: The University of Michigan, 1957.

The
MAN SOCIETY
TECHNOLOGY
Forum

C. Dale Lemons

Ecological imbalance, violence, production, diminishing energy reserves, overpopulation, unemployment, wasted human potential, cost of living increases, population mobility, loss of identity, drug abuse, pollution—terms among many currently being used to express dissatisfaction with technology and the use of technology in our society. An equal number of terms could be given to express the benefits that we enjoy as a result of technological development. In short, there appears to be strong conflict in opinions about the positive and negative effects of technology on man and his society. Daily you witness various attempts to escape the super-industrial society in which we live—anti-materialist groups, mystical cults, communes, reversion to by-gone eras in clothing, music, games, furniture, etc. This nostalgia may appear to be only a fad when in fact it represents an attempt to escape from the complexities of the technological culture in which we live.

Others attempt to function on a philosophy of nowness. Advertisements, songs, and life styles exemplify the "now generation." The demand for immediate gratification has pervaded college campuses, high school campuses, politics, minority groups, and touched all segments of our society.

Neither identification with the past nor locking-in on the present are viable alternatives. In this complex super-industrial age, the only alternative is to control or apply technology for the future benefit of man. It was on the premise of converting problems of technology to benefits for man that the forum project was founded. That is, it was felt that to use technology effectively it is necessary to develop what is referred to as technological literacy.

Further, in compliance with accepted definitions of industrial arts, the development of technological literacy is a concern of industrial arts. From Frederick Bonsor's definition, "a study of the changes made by man in the forms of materials to increase their values and of the problems of life related to these changes,"[1] to more contemporary attempts to define our discipline, there is reflected in a direct manner a responsibility for studying about the problems related to industrial and technological activity.

With varying degrees of success, attention has been given to a study of industry and technology, but little in industrial arts has been done to examine the resultant problems. Understanding technology and the relationships between this technology and society for the purpose of making rational decisions about the use of our technical knowledge is defined as technological literacy. Dr. John McKetta, in his presentation to the MAN/SOCIETY/TECHNOLOGY Mideast Forum, stated the charge in this manner: "All I ask is that you, because of your position and your ability and your knowledge in technical areas, provide calm, honest, intelligent information to your groups so that they can, when decisions are made, make the intelligent decision."[2] In this presentation, he was referring in part to industrial arts educators developing appropriate and correct concepts about technology in our society. The MAN/

SOCIETY/TECHNOLOGY Forum Project began with this primary focus.

Purpose of the Forum

Many misconceptions about the M/S/T forum series have been aired across the country. There are those who have criticized the project because they thought it to be an attempt to start another innovative program. Others judged the effort an attempt to move toward a more "academic" study and away from an activity-centered study. In both cases, as with several other notions about the purposes of the forum, these concepts were and are in error. In fact, the purposes of the forum project were so simple and fundamental that they were suspect.

The brochure which was sent to all AIAA members at the beginning of the forum series clearly identified the purposes of the forum.

First, the forum was to examine the promises and problems of technology as related to man and his environment with the focus on improvement of industrial arts programs and industrial arts teacher education. These promises and problems were not defined as being technical in nature, but were broadly identified as social, cultural, economic, and environmental concerns. Improvement of industrial arts programs was the primary goal for the industrial arts educators, but the other participants would have primary goals different than those of the profession. Therefore, emphasis was focused upon the concern for man and his environment—a common concern for all participants.

Second, in order to accomplish the first goal, dialogue had to be initiated and developed between industrial arts educators and others in education, and they in turn would communicate with persons from other segments of society. To be more specific, organized segments of our society were invited from the broad categories of government, labor, industry, and education. These groups were charged with analyzing the promises and problems of technology to extract implications for education.

Third, each forum was asked to analyze critically the goals of industrial arts to establish more clearly and firmly the relationship of industrial arts and technology. This task actually was to accomplish two purposes—that of communicating to participants the objectives and ambitions of industrial arts education and that of soliciting critical evaluation from the participants. The first in-depth discussion of our discipline to which many participants had been exposed occurred in the forum. The impact of this exposure will be discussed later in this article.

The fourth goal was to synthesize the promises and problems of technology with industrial arts education. It was anticipated that the broad representive mix of leadership personnel interacting in the forums would challenge the profession with startling new concepts about our role in the education of youth. However, many of the more forward thinkers in our field have already surpassed the collective recommendations of the forums. This is not to minimize the value of the results of the forum project. Many fine observations and recommendations were made—most of which were basic and fundamental; actions were called for to which we have given lip service but little else.

In the accomplishing of these goals, certain outcomes were expected. All these outcomes did not result to the extent desired, but it is better to set high goals and have to stretch than to set them too low and stoop. Among the outcomes expected were:

1. To establish an interdisciplinary base of labor, industry, government, and education to work more effectively on the promises and problems of technology.
2. To compile a list of resources to be utilized by faculty and students in industrial arts teacher education and the K-12 school program.
3. To develop a plan for implementing in each state an educational partnership to coordinate and utilize available resources effectively.
4. To develop recommendations for improving industrial arts programs and teaching at the elementary, secondary, and collegiate levels.

These were realized in varying degrees of success. Although not all results can be reported here, a portion of this article is devoted to reporting results of the forum series.

To accomplish the ideals as presented, it was imperative to have a plan that had a fair chance to succeed. The design or strategy of the forum series contributed largely to the success of the project. This strategy is briefly reviewed for your benefit.

Strategy

The strategy of the forum project was quite simple—to identify and involve leadership personnel from many segments of society in an interactive situation, around a topic of com-

FIGURE 1
COMMON CONCERN MODEL OF MAJOR SEGMENTS OF SOCIETY

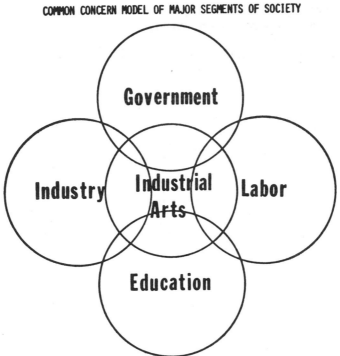

mon interest, to expand thinking, create interpersonal relationships, and result in recommendations and action for improved
educational programs. A model of this strategy might appear
as a number of overlapping circles where each circle would
represent the world of concern and resources of a given segment of society (Figure 1). The amount of overlap represents
areas of common interest and à basis for communication and
common effort. This model is certainly inadequate to effectively illustrate all possible combinations and amounts of
common interest; however, the concept is represented.

Although the premise of identifying and bringing together
persons of high caliber, leaders in their field whether in industry, government, labor, or education is a simple one to plan
and state, the accomplishment of the task is quite complex.
There were many factors affecting the success of such an
endeavor, of which planning was the most important.

In this planning, the following key points were given attention.

1. **Organization.** The organizational structure of personnel

attending to the many varied tasks of conducting the forums consisted of a Project Director, a Program Director, eight Regional Coordinators, and 98 State Coordinators [two from each state] (Figure 2), each operational level having specific duties necessary to the success of the venture.

FIGURE 2

STRUCTURE FOR REGIONAL M/S/T FORUMS

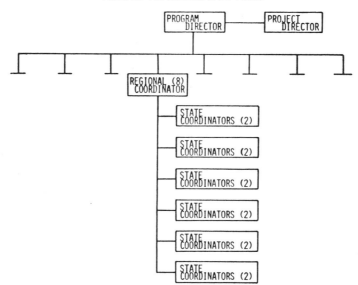

PROJECT DIRECTOR. The Project Director had the responsibility for managing fiscal matters and consulting with the Program Director concerning accomplishment of project goals.

PROGRAM DIRECTOR. The Program Director was responsible for identifying Regional and State Coordinators, informing them of their responsibilities, deadlines, goals, and mechanics of operation. He also identified speakers, locations, and other key individuals, usually in consultation with Regional Coordinators. Continued communications with all coordinators, preparation of program materials, invitational materials, and task assignments were all a part of this responsibility. Individual letters of invitation to all recommended participants as well as follow-up correspondence was handled through the office of the Program Director.

REGIONAL COORDINATOR. The Regional Coordinator had a very difficult task. In addition to acting as a stimulator to State Coordinators in his region, his responsibilities included making local arrangements with regard to housing, transportation, food, meeting rooms, recording equipment, registration of participants, and whatever local favors or information were available. One of the more difficult tasks of the Regional Coordinator was that of soliciting financial support from outside sources to help defray participant costs, and they did a fantastic job. The Regional Coordinators' duties did not end with these arrangements but also included responsibility for summarizing the forum proceedings and continuing to maintain communications and provide encouragement to the State Coordinators.

STATE COORDINATORS. The State Coordinators were key individuals in the success of a forum. It was their responsibility to identify the leaders in their state who would be interested in this endeavor, have input for the forum, attend, and interact with others from their respective states as well as other states. As the forum concept was centered on interaction between people, the type of individual involved was important. If you think that identifying leadership quality people from many different segments of society is not difficult, try compiling a list of 25 significant people equally distributed between government, labor, industry, and education. The State Coordinators also functioned as discussion leaders and recorders in the forums and were charged with continuing to serve as leaders in promoting similar action within their respective states.

2. **Program.** The program strategy was as critical a factor for success as personnel organization. The basic program design included three major topics with three types of activity structured within these divisions. The topic divisions were:

*An Examination of Technology/Society Relationship
*An Analysis of Educational Responsibility
*The Formulation of a Consortium.

In each of these divisions a presentation was made by a selected speaker to focus the participants' thinking on the topic. The presentations made follow in this issue of the journal. They had the effect of expanding or restricting concerns of the participants, and it is hoped that you will read these as a challenge to your philosophy and program. The presentations were followed by forum discussion of the topic, small group (six to ten participants) discussions with task assignments consistent with the topic and purposes of the forum, and reports from the groups to the forum for further discussion. There were many factors contributing to or hindering the success of any one regional forum; the most significant of these was human resources; that is, the caliber of participants, coordinators, and presenters. In addition to human resources, other significant factors were timing of the forum, location, facilities, communications by directors and coordinators, and commitment of leadership personnel.

To sum up the strategy, it started with goals; then, through careful planning, a program was developed that brought creative people together in an atmosphere conducive to constructive action.

Impact of the Forum: People

There were many benefits resulting from the forum series, the most important of which is the new friends made for industrial arts. In one way or another, the forum touched many people. In the eight regions, 926 persons were actually invited to participate; however, numerous others were formally or informally contacted. The geographical area covered and attendance in each regional forum is shown in Figure 3. Table 1 is an analysis of persons invited and participating.

Statistics, of course, reveal only quantitative data and do little to reflect the quality of individuals or the degree of impact made upon them. Even those who did not, by choice or because of conflicting schedules, participate in a regional forum were made aware of the concern industrial arts has for technology and society. This contact in itself can be significant.

To speak briefly about the quality of participants, a sampling of individuals participating from each category follows:
1. Government
    —State senator
    —Administrative heads from state government
    —Mayor
    —Federal agency heads
2. Labor
    —Labor commissioners
    —Union officials, state level
    —Union officials, local level
3. Industry
    —Presidents of companies
    —Presidents or officers of industrial organizations
    —Personnel managers
    —Chamber of commerce officials

46

—Educational supervisors of industry

4. Education
    —Superintendents of public instruction
    —Assistants to chief school administrator
    —College presidents
    —University professors of other disciplines
    —Local school superintendents

5. Students
    —Students of industrial arts on high school, college, and graduate levels

    —Students other than industrial arts—the quality of which may be judged from the following example. One young lady from a medium-sized state youth organization participated in one regional forum.

Table I
MAN/SOCIETY/TECHNOLOGY
PARTICIPANTS IN REGIONAL FORUMS

CATEGORY		SE	SC	WC	RM	MC	NC	NE	ME	TOTAL
GOVERNMENT	I	15	16	14	14	14	23	11	24	131
	A	*17	8	4	5	8	5	3	10	60
LABOR	I	9	6	4	7	9	21	6	6	68
	A	2	0	2	1	3	7	1	1	17
INDUSTRY	I	26	25	36	29	65	47	40	29	297
	A	4	7	12	18	11	9	7	12	80
EDUCATION	I	25	22	16	27	22	19	21	27	179
	A	5	12	7	12	8	10	6	11	71
INDUSTRIAL	I	18	23	27	21	19	24	22	24	178
ARTS	A	*19	24	18	22	19	23	23	24	172
STUDENTS	I	3	2	4	8	0	1	6	4	28
	A	2	2	4	7	0	1	2	4	22
OTHERS	I	6	5	5	4	3	9	3	10	45
	A	1	0	1	1	1	1	0	4	9

The FORUM columns are: SE SC WC RM MC NC NE ME

I—Invited
A—Attending
*NASA and M/S/T Personnel Included

Total Invited 926
Attending 431

47

Her involvement in the forum was so significant that at the final session she received a standing ovation from all participants. You can believe that this young lady will be a spokesman for industrial arts, although she had never taken a course.

Other
   —State and local school board members and chairmen
   —State and local PTA officials

In addition to regular participants, many of the speakers became thoroughly convinced of the value of industrial arts. Their names and positions are provided along with their presentation in this issue of the journal.

In addition to these outstanding individuals, the Educational Programs Officers of NASA centers should be recognized for their efforts and the tremendous support of the forum project. Dr. Fred Tuttle, Director of Educational Programs, NASA, Washington, D.C., provided leadership and support throughout the entire project and has become a strong advocate of industrial arts. Space does not permit me to name all of the NASA personnel involved in the project, but should anyone desire an educational program that concerns current technology, contact should be made with the nearest NASA center to ascertain what input can be provided.

While recognizing the contributions of people, recognition of the companies that supported the forum series not only in personnel but also with financing should be made and will be published.

Impact of the Forum: Action and Ideas

A few significant outcomes of the forum series in the form of ideas and actions should be mentioned. The ideas sometimes took the form of challenges or charges to our field, and the actions are continuing efforts to establish consortiums for the improvement of industrial arts.

As the forum series progressed, it was soon apparent that industrial arts was not unique in trying to promote cooperative and partnership efforts to improve education. A number of industry-education cooperation councils were discovered in operation, but industrial arts educators had not been involving themselves. A large number of community resources workshops have been conducted in various parts of the United States in which industry and education cooperated to make education more relevant in today's world. But, again, industrial arts teachers had not involved themselves. This represents

48

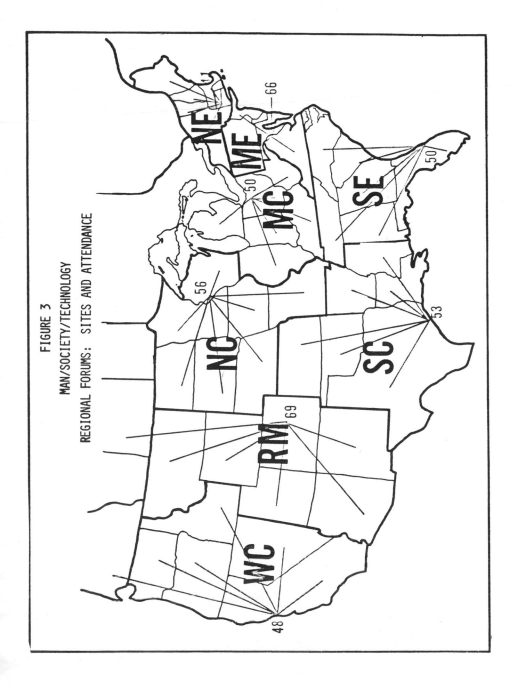

FIGURE 3

MAN/SOCIETY/TECHNOLOGY

REGIONAL FORUMS: SITES AND ATTENDANCE

a major challenge. We profess to teach about industry and the technology of industry, but do not avail ourselves of the opportunity to associate with the element which we claim as a source of subject matter. As a participant in one of the forums stated it, "The industrial arts teacher must get out of the shop occasionally and get involved in the community." This can accomplish two things; he can find out what is happening, and he can spread the good word about the contributions of industrial arts to the education of youth.

Speaking of spreading the word, a recurring observation in all of the forums was that the public relations efforts of industrial arts teachers were very poor, if not nil. As Boardman Moore put it, "You must tell the public what you are doing for their children."[3] The need for an organized, effective, and active public relations effort was made vividly clear in each forum. This is a challenge to every industrial arts teacher and more pointedly to state and local industrial arts organizations.

Perhaps the most often and universally agreed upon outcome of the entire series was the need for industry and education to cooperate to improve education. This was viewed as a two-way proposition where each would support the other. Further implied was the need for interdisciplinary studies— interdisciplinary in the broad sense, which would include the community as well as academic disciplines.

The following is a grocery list of statements made, with implications for if not direct charges to the industrial arts profession. These statements were selected from various forums and are intended to provide merely a sampling of the forum activity.

—Provide for the exposure of technology to pre-school children and continually throughout life.
—Develop within the pupil a positive attitude toward change and an acceptance of it.
—Energy sources and uses are not infinite, and technology can create an unreal or false sense of security.
—The use of educational facilities must and can be used more effectively.
—Pupils must understand economics of our society.
—What values and ethical goals could form the common denominator of a technological society to provide all people with a quality life?
—Schools should develop curricula that place more emphasis on "doing" rather than abstraction.

50

- —Colleges must break the "for young people only" syndrome and become centers of continuing education for people throughout their lives.
- —A study of technology must include not only the technical dimensions of technology but also the role of man and his relationship to a highly technological society.
- —There is a crying need to eliminate waste and to use by-products more effectively.
- —Should we think in terms of large content areas with a more comprehensive education rather than specialized content?
- —Education must cause young people to develop the ability to make intelligent judgements concerning material things.
- —Schools should prepare every child for leisure as well as for occupational competency.
- —Educational technology including multi-media and multi-activity instruction must be used more effectively.
- —Industrial arts, like many areas of education, has taught courses in isolation from the public and even from other educators and disciplines.
- —Place less emphasis on the subject name and image and greater emphasis upon the results desired from the program.

These are but a few of the hundreds of concerns and recommendations expressed. Where these represent the combined thinking of people from many segments of our society, it is wise to give serious attention to the message, if not folly to ignore it.

Where To from Here

The question might well be asked—okay, it sounds fine, but how? A few states have already made attempts to find out. Arizona and Pennsylvania have held state forums to touch base with local leaders and get them into the act. Several other states have devoted their annual state association meetings to a MAN/SOCIETY/TECHNOLOGY discussion and planning session. In other states, individuals and groups have begun to actively participate in industry-education cooperation councils. The possibilities are limited only by the imagination and the willingness of individuals and groups to work.

The question has been repeatedly asked, of what benefit has the forum been to the classroom teacher who must daily enter the laboratory to teach a group of students? It can be of significant value when the message of industrial arts is clearly communicated to the public to gain the support for improved programs. When a legislator, a school board member, a city official, an industrial leader, a labor leader, or an interested citizen knows what industrial arts can do to help people understand and cope with the technological society in which they live, an expensive program may appear much less costly.

The Regional Coordinators and the Directors of the project met in Washington after all eight forums were completed to evaluate the results and make recommendations for further action. Several categories were identified to which attention should be given:
—Funding and legislation to promote the discipline.
—Identification of outside resources.
—Organization of industrial arts personnel.
—Planning of activities.
—Planning of instructional programs.
While these may seem vague at first, reflection will reveal that these are the areas in which the profession has been weakest.

To help state and local industrial arts organizations, the AIAA will be printing guidelines to aid in the planning and operation of forum programs. Also, several articles and publications are planned to bring to the membership the results of the regional forums.

All in all, the Forum Project has been a successful venture—many new friends have been made and many of our practices have been challenged. I, personally, have benefitted greatly from the experience and plan to continue working to promote a consortium of industry and education. Let me end by saying, get involved—but think big and plan well. Be open, sincere, and willing to listen as well as speak out.

Footnotes

[1] Frederick Bonsor and Lois Mossman, *Industrial Arts for Elementary Schools* (New York: The MacMillan Company, 1942), p. 3.

[2] John McKetta, in an address ("Technology—Promises and Problems for Man and His Environment") at the Goddard Spaceflight Center, Greenbelt, Maryland, November 15, 1971.

[3]Boardman Moore, in an address ("The Four R's in the Educational Partnership") at the Ames Research Center, San Jose, California, March 2, 1971.

VOCATIONAL EDUCATION AS A SOCIAL MOVEMENT

SOCIAL CONDITIONS MUST CONTINUE TO BE THE MOTIVATION FOR CHANGE IN VOCATIONAL EDUCATION

MELVIN L. BARLOW

ONE OF THE principal arguments for vocational education is that it is a social necessity. In theory and in fact it represents an individual's turning point from economic dependency upon the social structure to his independent posture as a productive member of society. This transition can and does affect a person once or more times during his life. Vocational education is truly the bridge between man and his work.

Vocational education developed during the early years of the twentieth century out of the needs of people and this is still its major emphasis as we look toward implementation of the Vocational Education Amendments of 1968.

Although the basic emphasis remains constant, the ways and means of achieving the educational goal do change. That is, effectiveness of vocational education in meeting the needs of people depends upon how clearly social change is detected and how wisely this change can be served. In short, it is the nature of the contemporary social setting that has been, and must continue to be, the motivation for change in vocational education.

Consistent Element. In 1917, vocational education helped youth and adults find a more appropriate place in the world of work—a place better suited to their interests and abilities. A person could go to work easily in 1917 without special training, but vocational education made the difference between just a job, and a job for which the person had special aptitude and preparation.

Occupational mobility was enhanced because the person was able to "find himself" in productive life.

In 1969, the role of vocational education has changed from something that was good to something that is imperative. Without it, many young people cannot find work. With it, they can be included in vocational education's story of social success. The record contains countless examples of vocationally trained people moving from marginal productivity to an economic status which enables them to sample generously the benefits of society.

Historic Commitment. In principle and in theory, vocational education has had a commitment to *all* people. In 1907, it was intended that vocational education programs should be "open to all." Sex, creed, color or nationality should not debar anyone. This point of view—expressed in the proceedings of the National Society for the Promotion of Industrial Education ten years before the Smith-Hughes Act was passed—identified

the target goal of people to be served. This commitment was upheld vigorously by the Panel of Consultants on Vocational Education in 1961-62 and was supported without reservation by the Advisory Council on Vocational Education in 1967.

The Vocational Education Act of 1963 and the Vocational Education Amendments of 1968 declare again the basic purpose of vocational education: To improve and expand vocational programs "so that all persons of all ages in all communities will have ready access to vocational training or retraining which is of high quality, which is realistic in the light of actual or anticipated opportunities for gainful employment, and which is suited to their needs, interests, and ability to benefit from such training."

It is difficult to state the case in plainer language. It does say *all,* and it means *all.*

The contemporary social emphasis on vocational education did not develop as a crash response to the emotion-charged social environment of the sixties. The social emphasis has been a consistent element of the program of vocational education during the last half-century. But over and above this consistency of principle and purpose, the contemporary environment of deep social concern has caused vocational education to become much more sensitive to the vocational needs of more people in relation to a larger segment of the occupational world. Vast numbers of them—as the 1968 Amendments state—are disadvantaged students: "disadvantaged academically, socially, economically, and culturally."

As the Council Saw It. Because an occupation is the most occupying of all human activities, it sets the tone of social relationships. It is the major element influencing the standard of living; it is a factor in determining family solidarity; and it controls the quality and quantity of civic participation and responsibility.

The Advisory Council on Vocational Education, well aware of the quality and quantity of current vocational programs, stressed the importance of extending them to a larger segment of the student body. But it also emphasized the necessity to *seek out* other youth and adults who have fallen between the cracks of the educational system, victims of conditions whch they neither created nor have any control over, their plight a threat and a burden to society. To the Advisory Council, the social function of vocational education was clear: to help restore these dropouts—both young and adult—to their proper places in society.

The Advisory Council did not limit its social concern to the immediate situation of the person and his job. It also noted that it is important for the student to learn early in his educational career about the demands of work and the dignity of labor, and for these concepts to be incorporated into actual work experience as part of the student's educational program.

In the Council's view, the ultimate decision youth must make about work should be made on the basis of his practical knowledge of work together with knowledge of himself in relation to it.

Left to chance and natural evolvement, the potential talents of youth for the world of work emerge slowly. This fact constitutes both an economic and social loss, particularly when it is known that technological change is demanding specific preparation for entrance into the newer occupational spectrum.

Social Investment. Keeping youth in school in an educational program relevant to their life goals is a social advantage. Young people can make the transition from this educational environment to the world of work successfully when they can perform the work available. They can increase their mobility in the world of work if they have continuing access to an educational program directly related to their occupational needs.

As the Council saw it, the task was two-fold: on the one hand, to make training available in an atmosphere of educational relevancy; on the other, to find solutions to the financial problems of potential students.

A large portion of the costs of vocational education can be regarded as social investment—an investment with excellent prospects for society to recover the dollars expended as the vocationally prepared youth becomes a productive unit in the economy.

In some cases the financial problem is merely a matter of providing jobs for which youth can be paid so they can stay in school. But many young people need much more. Thousands of them will not be in school next year because they cannot begin to pay the educational and residential costs. Failure to provide these funds means a loss to society.

In every element of the Advisory Council's study, the social value of vocational education was apparent. The Council projected the services of vocational education deep into the social structure where they had never before been felt. Availability changed from "Here it is; come and get it," to "We will bring it to you."

Congress & the Amendments. The basis for long and continued support of vocational education by Congress is rooted in the recognition of vocational education as a social movement. This is clearly stated in the record of Congress at any time when vocational education has been under discussion in the Senate and the House of Representatives. The Vocational Education Amendments of 1968 are the most recent example of this Congressional concern. It is unequivocally indicated in the declaration of purpose of the Act, and it is further implied throughout the Act.

The Amendments of 1968 contain many provisions designed to safeguard the social objectives of vocational education. For example:

• National and state advisory councils are required to be representative of a broad spectrum of American life, thus preventing narrow consideration of the social and occupational needs of people.

• Definitions contained in the Act are broad and are stated to be inclusive rather than limiting.

• Authorized uses of federal funds make it possible to implement a total program in the interests of vocational students and society.

• State plans, projected into the future, are intended to keep the vocational education program dynamic and functional in relation to the unique needs of people in any state.

• Research provisions call attention specifically to the "special needs of youth."

• Residential school provisions hit hard at the dropout problem and youth's unemployment.

• The provisions for consumer and homemaking education place stress on social and cultural conditions and emphasize the dual role of homemaker and wage earner.

• Cooperative vocational education programs are intended to remove artificial barriers which separate work and education—barriers which have made it difficult for youth to enter productive life.

These are only a few of the specific references to the social context of vocational education as reflected in the Amendments of 1968. The Act recommends many other specific measures which recognize the strong social motive of vocational education.

Knowledge that this motive is sound and realistic is spreading rapidly throughout the nation. Representatives of state governments see in the continued development of vocational education an opportunity to remove the causes of dependency on welfare programs by providing the opportunity for people to become prepared for available jobs. Remedial programs, although imperative at times, do not provide significant and enduring impact in efforts to strengthen the social fabric of the nation.

Columnists such as Alice Widener and Sylvia Porter have pointed to the realism of vocational education in the stark social setting. They have written about self-fulfillment and self-discipline in work—characteristics which are developed in vocational education—and they see a better future when the nation gives due attention to the great majority of our youth and adults who do not now receive, as a part of public education, the occupational education they desire and

57

need.

View from the Senate. A far-sighted Senator stated the case for vocational education as a social movement thus:

"Mr. President . . . I wish to emphasize what I regard as the fundamental purpose underlying this whole measure, namely that it designs through federal effort to blaze a trail which the several states may follow toward greater industrial efficiency and better citizenship for our young men and young women. Its purpose is to stimulate and encourage stronger state action along educational lines, with the central idea of promoting that equality of opportunity which this country owes to all, rich and poor alike.

"In my judgment, the chief purpose of this bill is the formation of character and citizenship . . . good citizenship is an absolute sine qua non for the general welfare and the common good. I submit, Mr. President, that it can be achieved in no way so well as by vocational education—indeed it is probable that there is no other way in which it can be done at all.

"There is something wrong in any school system which drives the average boy away from school life at the very time when he should be beginning to realize the great importance of education; but that is just what our present system of education does.

"To say that it is the boy's fault is futile. It is the fault of the curriculum of our schools in that it repels rather than attracts the average boy; and we shall never change this until we introduce into our school system a greater measure of vocational education.

"In an educated and prosperous citizenship is our only safety. In my judgment, prosperity can only follow education, and the education which we offer must be the kind boys and girls will accept or it may as well not be offered.

"Vocational education, more than any other agency, will augment and intensify the desire for more knowledge. It will unquestionably arouse into action thousands of boys possessing latent ability and talent, and with their desires whetted for still greater knowledge. Every institution of learning now in existence will become the direct beneficiary of the joint action of the nation and the state in providing, as here proposed, a stable foundation upon which can be built a broader education."

These remarks presenting a broad social view of vocational education were made by Senator Carroll S. Page of Vermont in the Senate 53 years ago. They are as modern as tomorrow, for vocational education was planned as a response to social need and never before has this need been greater.

A Conceptual Curriculum for...

Industrial Arts and Occupational Education

ALBERT J. PAUTLER

■ This article is the result of a recent article, "A Conceptual Framework for Industrial Arts and Vocational Education." It was suggested that a follow-up article, attach a curriculum to the framework.

It will not suggest that vocational education and industrial arts should merge into occupational education. But a closer relationship between the two would achieve the best programs possible. Every attempt should be made to make the instruction as meaningful as possible to the learner. Both programs must be flexible enough to meet individual needs of each learner. If the student's major needs can best be served by industrial arts education then allow him to major in industrial arts. If he needs vocational education program, then let him follow that type. If a combination of both is necessary, then allow the student the opportunity to follow such a program.

The suggested framework embraces some of the traditional aspects but will also involve some change of emphasis on the part of secondary industrial arts programs and vocational programs. It is realized also, that types of vocational and industrial arts offerings and their availability are of major concern. Many details and problems, no doubt, would exist at the local level, but nevertheless, I present the framework for your consideration.

Before considering the operational aspects of this conceptual curriculum let us describe each of the blocks making up the framework.

Youngsters in the elementary grades need a basic understanding and appreciation of the industrial technology and culture of America. If at all possible, some form of industrial arts education should be available at this level. The basic foundation of an elementary industrial arts program should be of value in later occupational decision making. Program organization, staff and curriculum can vary depending upon the local school district administration. Current literature on elementary industrial arts should be of value to program planners. (2, 3, 4)

Junior High School Industrial Arts

Industrial arts at the junior high school level should be able to perform a worthwhile service to all students. Both boys and girls should find an interest in learning about industry. The value to the student should be of help in later occupational decision making. A well organized industrial arts program at the junior high school level should help prepare students for secondary vocational-technical programs.

The content of courses at this level should be derived from a study of modern industry, with its ever-changing technology. An honest attempt should be made to get the *industry* back into industrial arts and leave the woods, metals, plastics and ceramics as the means of doing it. The changes we can expect in the years ahead are a consideration for all educators but should be of considerable importance to occupational educators. (5)

Various arrangements and scheduling for junior high programs exist and the most suitable to the local situation should be used. Room for program innovations certainly exists at the junior high school level and should be a challenge to industrial arts teachers. (2, 6)

Perhaps the most valuable place for a strong industrial arts program is in the junior high school. It is at this level that industrial arts in many states is a required course. Since this is the case, the influence of a workable and valuable program of industrial arts should be evident at the junior high school level.

60

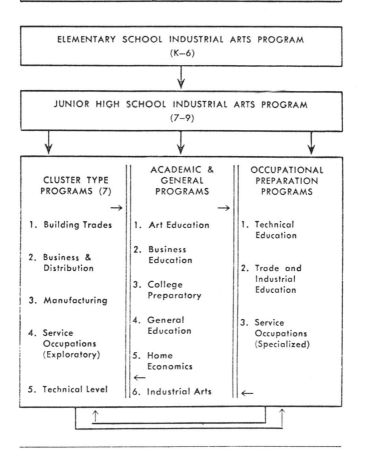

A CONCEPTUAL CURRICULUM IN OCCUPATIONAL EDUCATION

ELEMENTARY SCHOOL INDUSTRIAL ARTS PROGRAM
(K–6)

JUNIOR HIGH SCHOOL INDUSTRIAL ARTS PROGRAM
(7–9)

CLUSTER TYPE PROGRAMS (7)	ACADEMIC & GENERAL PROGRAMS	OCCUPATIONAL PREPARATION PROGRAMS
1. Building Trades	1. Art Education	1. Technical Education
2. Business & Distribution	2. Business Education	
	3. College Preparatory	2. Trade and Industrial Education
3. Manufacturing	4. General Education	
4. Service Occupations (Exploratory)	5. Home Economics	3. Service Occupations (Specialized)
5. Technical Level	6. Industrial Arts	

Senior High School

The major concern of this article is at the senior high school level. If available, an elementary industrial arts program is valuable to all students. Industrial arts programs are required in many junior high schools and serve a worthwhile purpose. The suggested progression would be from elementary to junior high school industrial arts and then to the senior high school program.

After junior high school I suggest three programs be made available for the students: 1) Academic and General Programs: This would include art, business, home economics and industrial arts programs. 2) A Cluster Program: "Cluster concept is a descriptive term applied to a form of vocational education directed toward the preparation of individuals for entrance into a spectrum of occupations." (7) 3) An Occupational Preparation Program which would include technical, trade and industrial, and service type occupations. A description of each of the three suggested programs follows.

Academic and General Programs

The more traditional types of programs will be found in this category. Academic is used to identify courses that are primarily intended to prepare students for further study in a given field, particularly in a post-high school area of specialization. General is used to identify those courses that are intended to prepare students either for post-high school study, or to provide basic preparation in a given area, or a number of different areas.

As indicated in the conceptual curriculum design, students should be able to move into cluster type programs or occupational preparation programs. Industrial arts programs at this level can help provide the students with necessary experiences on which to base occupational career choices. This holds true for the other areas listed under academic and general programs as well. Likewise, if a student desires to major in art education or industrial arts as part of the general program, he or she should be able to do so.

Cluster Type Programs

The cluster program would allow the student who is mainly interested in preparing for employment but not sure of the specialization, an opportunity to prepare for a range of occupations. (7) This type of program could follow after the junior high school program of industrial arts or it could be taken after the student has taken some high school level industrial arts courses. Of and by itself, it should be able to provide a student with some entry level skills to enter a group of occupations. The level of skill development would not approach that provided by the *occupational preparation program.*

The advantages of a cluster type program would be: 1) multi-occupational in the sense that it could prepare students for a group of occupations; 2) would allow students an opportunity to investigate a number of occupations within a cluster and decide on a specialization in the more advanced occupational preparation program; 3) serve a useful purpose in screening or selection of students for the more advanced specializations available in the occupational preparation programs.

The work and investigations of Dr. Donald Maley dealing with the cluster concept would be of great concern to program planners. (7)

I see a cluster type program in this conceptual curriculum in the following manner, using the building trades as an example. It is a multi-occupational program involving carpentry, electrical, heating, plumbing, painting, etc. The teacher would spend a certain amount of time dealing with each sub-specialization. Better yet, if the schedule could be arranged, allow students in the program to spend a certain amount of time in each of the building trades specialization. To rotate or spend one period per day with the occupational preparation instructors in carpentry, heating and plumbing is one example.

Much room for curriculum experimentation and various methods of providing cluster type programs should be considered. The final decision would be based upon the local situation. Do not rule out a program because it might create a scheduling problem. If our main concern is the student, our main objective should be to provide a sound program designed to attract and hold students until graduation. The cluster type program may be one answer in lowering the dropout rate from vocational specializations.

Occupational Preparation Programs

This would be similar to traditional vocational education programs. The term, occupational preparation, is used since programs in this category should lead to occupational competency and employment.

In this structure would be: 1) technical education, 2) trade and industrial education and, 3) service occupation programs.

Typical examples of each would be: 1) *Technical* — electrical technology, chemical technology, mechanical technology, computer technology, etc. 2) *Trade and Industrial* — carpentry, plumbing, electrical maintenance, automotive mechanics, etc. 3) *Service Occupations* —

63

food service, hotel and motel, waiter-waitress, nurses aid, child care, recreation, service station attendant, etc.

The supportive aspects of both the industrial arts and the cluster programs could benefit the occupational preparation program in both skill development and vocational choice of the students.

Many practical considerations would be necessary to implement a program of this nature. This is left to the industrial arts and vocational-technical educators at the local level. Program improvement and the implementation of new ideas must start at the local level. Evaluation should follow to determine the success or failure of the concept.

Bibliography

1. Pautler, Albert J., *A Conceptual Framework for Industrial Arts and Vocational Education*. Industrial Arts and Vocational Education, November, 1967.
2. Olson, Delmar W., *Industrial Arts and Technology*. Englewood Cliffs, New Jersey. Prentice-Hall, Inc., 1963.
3. Hunt, Elizabeth, "The Role of Industrial Arts in the Development of the Elementary School Child," *New Directions for Industrial Arts*. Addresses and Proceedings of the 26th Annual Convention of the American Industrial Arts Association. Washington: American Industrial Arts Association, 1964.
4. University of the State of New York. *Industrial Arts Education*. Albany, New York: The State Education Department, 1960.
5. Staff of the Wall Street Journal. *Here Comes Tomorrow! Living and Working in the Year 2000*. Princeton, New Jersey. Dow Jones Books, 1967.
6. Miller and Smalley. *Selected Readings for Industrial Arts*. Bloomington, Illinois: McKnight & McKnight Publishing Company, 1963.
7. Maley, Donald. *The Cluster Concept*. American Vocational Journal, October, 1967, pp. 22–23.

VOCATIONAL EDUCATION

AT THE CROSSROADS

Lowell A. Burkett

W^{E} ARE NOW APPROACHING the end of the Golden Anniversary Year of federal aid to vocational education. Fifty years ago there was a great manpower shortage in our country. Immigration laws had stopped the flow of artisans and craftsmen to the United States. Technology was beginning to advance.

Many people, including outstanding leaders of the day, were saying that education must expand to include vocational training; that vocational education was "socially efficient"; that the end of all schools must be life; that everybody in the nation must be taught to work; and that our farmers must have scientific education.

Enough interest was aroused to attract the attention of President Woodrow Wilson and the U. S. Congress. As a result, the Smith-Hughes Act became law and federal funds were provided for vocational education.

With the institutionalizing of vocational education, strong leadership for vocational education developed at all levels. And, for the first time, vocational education became a part of the public school system. There was also established at this time a federal-state-local structure for implementing programs of vocational education, both at the high school and adult levels.

Vocational education at the federal level was administered by a Federal Board for Vocational Education. Membership was made up of the Secretaries of Agriculture, Commerce, Labor, and the Commissioner of Education, plus three members appointed by the President and confirmed by the U. S. Senate. The composition of this Board set the pattern for states and local communities.

Let us briefly assess where we stand now with respect to some of these very basic and fundamental concepts in vocational education.

There is a revival of interest in vocational education throughout the nation. Certainly, we see much evidence of this interest in Washington. The federal investment in vocational education and training in fiscal year 1968 is approximately $2 billion. Let me point out, however, that of this amount only $400 million is allocated for expenditure through the federal-state-local structure created for the purpose of providing vocational education for America's citizens. Countless new agencies and organizations are being created by the federal government to provide vocational-technical education.

And what is happening at the state level? The same pattern. We find separate boards administering the high school program, the area vocational schools, and the community junior colleges. From the federal level right down to the state and local levels, there is no structure for coordinating, planning, and implementing a total program.

Within the Department of Health, Education, and Welfare, there is a Division of Vocational-Technical Education which is a part of the Bureau of Adult, Vocational and Library Programs. The Division is so low in the bureaucratic structure that no one from vocational education is present when national policies are formulated which ultimately affect what each of us does at the state and local level.

Millions of dollars are being programed for expenditure in the name of vocational education, and ambitious plans are being made to revamp and change vocational education. Much of this is being done without regard for experimentation or consultation with vocational educators. Nor is it supported by research evidence.

Position papers and status reports contain statements about vocational education which no one from vocational education has had a hand in preparing or an opportunity to question. These reports are fed into the information stream with the result that many decisions made about vocational education are based on information that is misleading, half fact, and in many instances, completely incorrect. Here is what I mean:

Last year the Council of Economic Advisers, a very

eminent and scholarly group, transmitted to Congress and to the President, its annual message which stated:

"Since its inception, the Job Corps has provided training and work experience for 61,500 of the most disadvantaged youths. When first enrolled more than 50 percent of the Job Corps enrollees failed to read at the 5th grade level, and 30 percent could not read a simple sentence. Despite this handicap, *the retention rate for the Job Corps is superior to that of vocational training programs nationally.*" (Italics added.)

When I wrote to question this statement, I received the following answer: "Unfortunately, the information we received was not accurate and we apologize for not catching this error in our fact-checking process. I am sorry if our treatment of this subject in the Economic Report has caused you any difficulty."

Another report, circulated in the Office of Education, stated:

"Of all secondary programs, vocational programs have the highest dropout rates. . . . The lack of holding power of vocational programs for low ability and poor socioeconomic students lessens the employment opportunities available to students who enroll in these programs.

"Fast-growth occupations in the economy are generally filled with high school graduates. The inability of vocational programs to retain students until graduation places students in these programs at a competitive disadvantage with other secondary programs."

These are some examples of the kind of information that is fed every day to the policymakers in Washington. It is this kind of information that we, as a professional association, must challenge and refute. Thus far, we have no evidence that the leadership in the Department of Health, Education, and Welfare is seeking to set the record straight.

Nor do we see any effort on the part of the Department of Health, Education, and Welfare to exert strong leadership in the field of vocational education and manpower development. For example, the Vocational Education Act of 1963 called for the appointment of a National Advisory Committee on Vocational Education, representative of education, business, industry, agriculture, and labor.

The Committee is supposed to advise the Commissioner of Education with respect to administration and other matters affecting vocational education. Do you know how many times that Committee met during 1967? Only once, and then it met jointly with the Advisory Council on Vocational Education, with no specific agenda of its own.

At the present time, there are four unfilled vacancies on the Committee.

While the summer fires flared and riots ravaged our land; while the schools continue to lose one third of their students each year; with 30 percent of the people in America's ghettos unemployed; with employers daily issuing ads of "help wanted"; with the certainty that unskilled jobs will continue to disappear; with a consistently increasing need for teachers of all types; with the shortage of medical technicians and health workers so drastic that treatment for the sick and chronically ill is gravely impaired; with the knowledge that only 20 percent of our school students will ultimately complete four years of college, together with the fact that only one fourth of our high school population is enrolled in vocational education —with all these facts screaming out at us daily from the newspapers and the television screens, there is not sufficient interest in Washington to call an advisory committee together to find ways and means to mobilize the forces in vocational education to make an impact on these problems.

The lack of commitment to vocational education is evident in other ways. For example, last June Congress passed a law providing funds for the training of educational personnel which required the establishment of a National Council of Education Professions Development. The function of the Council is to review programs and make recommendations to the Commissioner of Education regarding teacher education programs funded under the Act.

AVA has been actively working for such legislation for vocational education, and we have diligently presented our needs to the Congress. As a result, the House Committee, in reporting the legislation, stated:

"The Committee is gravely concerned about the inadequacy of support for training of persons serving or preparing to serve in vocational education programs. More than in any other case, the Committee was tempted to earmark a specific reservation of funds for training in this area. The Committee has not earmarked funds only because of its desire to establish a flexible program. Nevertheless, the Committee fully expects that the most serious attention and consideration will be given to support of training programs for vocational education teachers."

Of the 15 individuals appointed to advise the Commissioner of Education on training programs for educational personnel, not a single one of them is, or has ever been, directly involved with vocational education. Insofar as the effective preparation of vocational education personnel is concerned, I cannot be optimistic about the outcome of this legislation.

Caught in a Bureaucratic Framework

In discussing this breakdown of federal leadership for vocational education, I want to emphasize that I do so with complete objectivity insofar as personalities are concerned. I want to be the first to say that the employees of the Department of Health, Education, and Welfare are individuals of good character, rare dedication, and infinite good will. They are simply caught in a bureaucratic framework where there is no visibility for vocational education.

We are in a period of crisis in vocational education. We lack leadership at all levels, and most especially at the federal level. As we stand at the crossroads, we seem inclined to move in many directions at once. Vocational education today has many spokesmen but few statesmen.

What are we going to do about this crisis in leadership?

As we ponder this question, let us now think for a few moments about the second issue with which we are confronted: How much real progress have we made since 1962 when the Panel of Consultants dramatically spelled out the groups of people who were in urgent need of vocational instruction? How well have we carried out the Vocational Act mandate to serve people rather than programs.

There can be no question that significant progress has been made. We can look with satisfaction to expanding numbers of new area vocational schools and community college programs. We see broadened curriculum offerings, expanded opportunities for vocational teacher education, important developments in research and experimentation, and expanded State Department of Education services. But if we measure our accomplishments in terms of what still needs to be done, there can be little room for complacency.

We live in a time when a sound educational base is becoming essential for success in virtually all types of jobs. In addition, workers must have ready access to job-related upgrading and retraining in order to keep up with technological changes. We can no longer afford a piecemeal approach to vocational instruction for our young people and adults. Stopgap measures and token efforts cannot be tolerated. It is clear that our Nation must now have a *permanent, universal, continuing program of vocational education, readily available to all persons of all age groups and levels of ability, wherever they may live.*

To truly serve all people in all communities will call for significant new levels of federal support and federal leadership. The problem is too immense and too general to be left to local initiative alone. But it must be clear: **no truly effective permanent change can be made in our** educational process without a full measure of local involvement and participation. National leadership is necessary in the articulation of our major purposes, and in setting standards for evaluation; but the implementation of these into actual programs of activity and operation must be carried out by the states and local communities —actually, by the individual teacher.

How much planning have you done in your state toward the goal of providing vocational education opportunities for all persons, of all ages, in all communities? Do you have a five-year plan, a ten-year plan? Is the community involved in planning? Have you established advisory committees?

Has your state vocational association recommended to your governor, and to your state legislature, a legislative program to implement your goals? What are you doing to create public support for your program? Does your state have a public information officer for vocational education? Does your state vocational association give leadership and direction to the program in your state and promote the professional growth of its members?

And now, we come to our last point. What new directions will AVA take during the coming year? How can we best use our resources to meet the critical challenges of leadership and program expansion and development? Where can we get the additional resources that will be necessary if we are to successfully pursue our course? What will our agenda for action be?

The recommendations of the Advisory Council on Vocational Education are now being printed, and will be presented to the Secretary of Health, Education, and Welfare and to the President and the Congress. Each will review the recommendations and will no doubt propose a plan for action.

In reality, however, it is up to us who work as professionals in the field of vocational education to implement these recommendations. And AVA is prepared to take some definite steps.

As a beginning, your Board of Directors has authorized us to embark on an enlarged communications program, both within our own professional ranks and with all our various publics. A communications program necessitates a permanent and massive research effort.

AVA will undertake the task of collecting information regarding the scope and range of our national vocational education program. Such information will bring into focus the problems and issues relating to vocational education. It will call attention to significant new developments and illustrate the sources of strength in vocational schoolwork.

It can highlight the ingredients that have made this form of education a truly vital force in our society and it can bring about a better understanding of vocational education's role in the total program of education.

Perhaps equally important, we will have facts to combat some of the erroneous information that is being circulated about vocational education.

AVA is also committed to strengthening and expanding its role in working with state vocational associations. We must create a constant flow of information to and from our state affiliates. State associations must sponsor leadership development programs, help collect information about vocational education, and promote standards in our various vocational fields.

It is through professional activities of the state associations that we must meet the challenge of providing vocational education for all people in all communities of all ages—for it is they who have the power to bring it about. By working together in a national organization, state vocational associations can bring to reality the permanent, universal, continuing program of vocational education about which we spoke earlier.

And I must remind you that your national association is no stronger or no weaker than the state associations which form it.

Our new organizational structure will open the way for many new people to become identified with AVA. All states must move toward opening their membership to *all persons* engaged in vocational-technical and practical arts education.

And let us all remember that our problems will be those that challenge all of vocational education and all vocational educators. We must not be so prone to think of our own specialties. It is important for us, of course, to know and understand and promote our own programs. After all, we do not teach vocational education—we teach for an occupation. But for too long we have tended to have vested interests in our occupational specialties, and this has deterred the total program of vocational education.

As vocational educators we have made some important contributions to American education. We have represented that part of education which emphasizes applied learning. We have promoted the practical aspects of education.

Very early we identified ourselves with the idea that learning is continuing—that it does not stop at some magic age of 18, or at high school graduation. We recognized the fact that people learn at many stages in life and that the desire for gainful employment and the practical aspects of vocational education often motivate individuals to achieve beyond their own or their teacher's expectations.

Vital Forces That Must Be Kept

Vocational educators have also stressed the idea of using the resources of the community and the home to provide a program of education. We have used the resources of the business community as an extension of the classroom; we have involved ourselves in the homes and on the farms of our students to help them create a more productive and satisfying environment; and we have sought the help and cooperation that is necessary to provide a realistic program of occupational training. We must not lose these vital forces from American education.

Each of us will have to work harder and do more to promote our profession than we have ever done before. We will have to devote time to the task. We may even have to raise the dues we pay for membership in our professional organization.

These are decisions that you will have to make. It is going to be left to the profession to meet these very serious challenges. We cannot expect others to do this job for us.

I have great faith in vocational education and in the professional people who work in the field. I have no doubt that we will provide the resources that will be needed.

THE

PHILOSOPHY

EDUCATION FORGOT

concepts for the education of the noncollege bound

Milton E. Larson

EIGHT HUNDRED of every thousand young people complete formal education without a college degree. For many, employment becomes the goal without realistic preparation for wage earning. Students who were not ready to make an occupational choice while in school are forced to suffer the consequences of poor or no formal preparation for their biggest and most far-reaching decision— their lifework.

Why does this happen? How can the richest and in many ways the most advanced nation in the world tolerate such mishandling of its human resources? Is there a relationship between the prevalent philosophy of education in the United States and the lack of preparation of non-college-bound youth for the role which statistics tell us most of these citizens will play in life?

Concepts of philosophy form the springboard for action. With $11 billion budgeted for fiscal year 1968 for education, training, and allied pro-grams by the federal government alone, the time seems ripe for reassessment of educational philosophy.

In the words of a great philosopher: "What is obviously needed is a truly liberal academic community in which the study of art and typewriting, of philosophy and accounting, of theology and medicine, of pure and applied science, are, though admittedly very different, judged to be equally honorable and valuable in their several ways."[1]

And the now famous quote from John W. Gardner: "The society which scorns excellence in plumbing because plumbing is a humble activity and tolerates shoddiness in philosophy because it is an exalted activity

---

[1] Greene, Theodore M. "A Liberal Christian Idealist Philosophy of Education," *Modern Philosophies and Education.* Fifty-Fourth Yearbook, Part 1, National Society for the Study of Education. Chicago: University of Chicago Press, 1955. Ch. 4, p. 119.

will have neither good plumbing nor good philosophy. Neither its pipes nor its theories will hold water."[2]

Educational Determinants. Determinants of educational philosophy today are many and varied. Can it be true that our pipes hold water better than much of the philosophy which forms the base for many of the practices of education and educators?

Has the concept of a "status occupation" in the minds of parents and youth alike excessively influenced decisions in education? Has the restricted personal experiences of many of the educational policy-makers resulted in failure to focus on realities of life? Has the "procrastinators' club" infiltrated education too?

Decision making is a learned process. The educational environment as well as the home influence can enhance or retard the ability of youth to make decisions concerning occupational choice. Are youth being equipped to make decisions of this scope at the most desirable time? Are they being provided the tools vital to the task of decision making?

In a world where scientific knowledge doubles every 10 years, an eighteenth-century educational philosophy is obsolete. Education for occupations must be at least as important as education for avocations, and education for employment as important as education for recreation. Education for wage earning must be at least as important as education for appreciation of the dynamic life of the sixteenth century as reflected in the literature of that day.

A new yardstick is essential. Need and service, reality and functionalism, and time and money available for acquiring salable competencies must be brought into focus. Time is a

² Gardner, John W. "Quality in Higher Education," *Current Issues in Higher Education.* Washington, D.C.: Association for Higher Education, 1958.

valuable component.

Employers no longer simply ask, have you gone to high school? Have you gone to college?

What have you learned that I can use if I employ you? This is the expressed or implied question in the minds of employers who are buying labor.

The choice of curriculum is a factor in the development of salable competencies. A curriculum of quality is essential to the preparation of youth for the world of reality beyond the formal door marked "Education." Quality spells the difference between mediocre and outstanding employment performance.

Quality education can be had only for the price of quality education. Buying education is like buying merchandise; we get only what we pay for.

Achieving Quality. Quality education for noncollege-bound youth results from the efforts of quality administrators, supervisors, and coordinators working with quality guidance personnel and teachers to produce a quality product—youth bound for employment that is personally satisfying and adequately rewarded financially.

Quality education for noncollege-bound youth results from a balanced curriculum of vocational and general education courses. The vocational curriculum must be sufficiently concentrated in one area to provide employable "depth." It must have enough breadth in related areas of vocational education to provide for inevitable changes of vocations and for variety in employer demands.

The vocational curriculum must not only be built on a solid foundation of applicable general education, it must be constantly integrated with it. The biggest challenge facing general education today is to make education meaningful to those exposed to it. Quality education for noncol-

74

lege-bound youth, as for the college bound, must be meaningful.

But for the noncollege-bound, it cannot be purely general in nature. Education for these young people must reflect the requirements of specific occupational clusters realistically taught. This means teachers who not only know about work but who have actually experienced what they are teaching to others.

It means adequate equipment similar to that used in actual work places and it means an environment of physical facilities designed not only for storage of equipment but also for a climate conducive to learning for employment.

Quality education for noncollege-bound youth means providing enough time in vocational courses for adequate preparation.

Noncollege-bound youth rarely lack ability, but frequently lack motivation. They rarely lack time to acquire marketable competencies, but often lack the challenge to make something of their lives.

Quality education for noncollege-bound youth must reflect the employer's needs. It must magnify to the student his opportunities in a selected field of occupation though he never earns a "sheepskin." It must give meaning to the expression "learning is a continuous process." Today no education is terminal.

Must Be Purposeful. Quality education for noncollege-bound youth must be designed to meet their needs, purposes, and objectives. Otherwise it is not quality education for them.

To repeat in part Mr. Gardner's statements relative to a discussion of quality junior college education:

"The traditionalist might say, 'Of course. Let Princeton create a junior college and one would have an institution of unquestionable excellence! That may be correct, but it leads us down precisely the wrong path. If Princeton Junior College were excellent in the sense that Princeton University is excellent, it might not be excellent in the most important way that a community college can be excellent. A comparable meaningless result would be achieved if General Motors tried to add to its line of low-priced cars by marketing the front half of a Cadillac."[3]

Too often the preparation of the noncollege-bound youth for the world of work is the equivalent to the front end of a Cadillac. (Many employers refrain from investing in front ends of Cadillacs.)

The result of such training is a product (student) difficult to market and hence another potential human resource destined for unemployment, crime, and drain on the financial resources of society, or at best, a prime candidate for the Job Corps centers and MDTA training programs.

Emphasis on the Real. Generally speaking, noncollege-bound youth are a breed different from the college-bound. The difference is evident not only in terms of aspirations but also in the approach to decision making and problem solving. Emphasis on hardware rather than theory is typical; desire for meaningful activities now rather than abstractions is frequently the case. Success in school is important.

Success comes from the ability to perform and the confidence resulting from previous success. Meaningful "doing" is vital to such success. Football players learn by doing; band members build harmony through practice; students in driver training classes need cars to drive. Long-distance swimmers acquire skill, competence, and confidence through many hours of practice under the guidance of a master.

---

[3] *Ibid.*

75

For the noncollege-bound, maturity for the task ahead results only from similar coaching and practice under actual conditions, much repetition, and the vision of success inspired by an educational climate dedicated to produce winners in the field.

Is it any wonder that about two thirds of all workers who never complete high school are employed in unskilled and semi-skilled jobs? That unemployment among young people 16 to 21 years of age is two to three times higher than in the rest of the labor force? That our educational system during the 1960's has produced some 7.5 million dropouts equipped with few if any job qualifications?

Greatest Resource. Can a nation continue to be great and at the same time fail so many people? America's greatest resource is her human resource.

As Grant Venn stated recently:

"The DuPont Company could lose every factory and every piece of capital investment that they have and still be one of the great corporations in this country if they could keep the people on their present work force. If they lost the people who are working for them, they would break up in three months. Wealth no longer lies in goods and materials. Today, real wealth lies in the minds of creative and imaginative individuals."[4]

Hope for the noncollege-bound youth lies in a new and enlightened concept of the purpose of total education for all American youth. A revised philosophy, broad enough to provide realistically and in meaningful terms for the real needs of all, including the noncollege bound, offers tremendous returns for our nation—financial, social, and psychological.

America has the resources to accomplish this broad educational task, but do the individuals who determine educational policy have the philosophy essential to implement such programs at the level of need?

[4] Venn, Grant. "Needed: A New Relationship Between Education and Work." *School Shop*, XXIV (April 1965), pp. 43-45, 106.

WHAT
IS
QUALITY VOCATIONAL
EDUCATION?

Burr D. Coe

I AM DEEPLY concerned about many things I see going on in the name of vocational education. Like many others, I have deep convictions, based on years of experience, about what sound, high-quality vocational education really is. Recognizing that having convictions can sometimes get you convicted, I propose to spell out my ideas about quality vocational education.

Those who have devoted a professional lifetime to vocational education do not need to be told that vocational education before the passage of the 1963 Act was a limited program, served far too few who needed vocational education, often was housed in inadequate and outdated facilities, and operated on a financial starvation diet.

Why do you suppose we worked so hard to get the 1963 Act passed? It was our great hope for the years ahead. It was to be our chance to do better what we already knew how to do and to find new ways to reach more people. We knew full well that there must be financial help if schools were to be built. The need for sound research and long-range evaluative studies was all too evident.

But some of the things now happening are not quite what we had in mind.

In our present drive to reach more students we may be hurting them more than helping them. Many programs are based on unsound principles, taught by occupationally unqualified teachers, and hastily structured to take instant advantage of federal funds.

Haste Makes Waste

There are real dangers in moving too fast. It takes time and a lot of planning to develop good, high-quality programs. It cannot be done overnight. And if in our haste we encourage unsound programs, who gets hurt? Mostly the students we mean to help.

When we were working on the development of the 1963 Act, one of the criteria often and emphatically stressed was that it must be *quality* vocational education. The first paragraph of the Declaration of Purpose uses the phrase "vocational training or retraining which is of high quality." I well remember Dr. M. D. Mobley telling us that Congress would insist that it be *quality* vocational education; and if it were not, we would be in deep trouble when we sought Congressional support.

What is quality vocational education? I firmly believe that quality vocational education must be based on the following principles:

1. *A quality program prepares students for entry into a chosen occupation without neglecting the essentials of a sound general education.*

There *must* be an employment objective; otherwise the program is a program *about* vocations; it is not preparation *for* a vocation. Vocational education is based on the essentials of a good general education but not a part of it. The strength of vocational education is in its dedication to its employment objective and close working relationships with employers and labor. If vocational education loses its separate identity and becomes absorbed in general education, it is a ship without a rudder and will be lost.

2. *A quality program is flexible; it permits youth and adults to enter into training when ready and able to do so.*

We must fit the program to the student, not the student to the program. Vocational education stresses individualized instruction, based on each pupil's unique abilities and goals. It has adjustment capability.

3. *A quality program accepts the responsibility for the retraining of unemployed and underemployed workers, upgrading of employed workers, related instruction for apprentices, and other types of vocationally oriented adult education opportunities and services.*

Vocational education has a major responsibility to be available throughout the working lifetime of our people. It is not and never has been confined to pre-employment training.

Counselor's Role

4. *A quality program provides for a wide variety of exploratory and occupational information opportunities. It helps students make wise choices for further education and training, helps them find satisfactory employment, and remains available for further counseling service during the working lifetime of the individual.*

Good vocational guidance counselors are a necessity in a total program; but they must have sufficient work experience and knowledge of the world of work to be able to realistically advise students. This process can begin earlier than high school, provided the student is free to make his own ultimate occupational and educational choices.

5. *A quality program is administered and supervised by personnel who are educated and experienced in vocational education, who understand the needs of pupils and the needs of business and industry, and who are able to work effectively with employers, labor, other school officials, and employment and social agencies.*

Some of the present problems in vocational education have been created by well-meaning people who lack sufficient experience in vocational education to develop and maintain quality programs. There is real danger when such persons also have the power and authority to make far-reaching decisions.

6. *A quality program serves a geographic area whose student population is large enough to support a day and evening program offering a wide variety of occupational choice and that has employment opportunities related to the training given.*

One of the greatest weaknesses of the comprehensive high school is that it is usually too small to provide a sufficient variety of vocational programs. Unless it is a very large school, it never can be truly comprehensive. The area vocational school often provides the best solution to this problem.

7. *A quality program is housed in physical facilities which are adequate, well-planned, and properly equipped to provide realistic vocational education.*

To many people a shop is a shop. Changing the name over the door does not make it vocational education. Existing non-vocational programs doing a good job should be encouraged and expanded; they should not be converted simply because federal funds are available for vocational education.

8. *Teachers in a quality program are masters in their occupation and have completed teacher-training programs where they have learned how to impart their knowledge and skills to pupils.*

How can a teacher properly prepare a student for entry into an occupation unless he has had experience in that occupation? But teaching is also an occupation to be learned.

Occupational Analysis

9. *A quality program is based on an analysis of each occupation to determine what is required to perform as a successful worker in that occupation.*

It is not enough to make an occupational analysis once; the analysis must be constantly updated. More than knowledge and skills is involved; responsibility, good working habits, and relationships with fellow workers and employers must also be taught.

10. *A quality program adjusts its curriculum to changing business and industrial conditions, technological change, and the requirements of the labor market. It properly uses advisory committees to assist in this process.*

Active advisory committees in close and regular contact with the program at the operating level can be extremely helpful and a source of strong support for a program. The closer they are to the instructional process the more valuable they are to the program and the more active and constant is their interest.

11. *A quality program provides for the learning of the skills employed in using the tools, machines, and materials of the occupation and using them safely, with good judgment, and with pride in good workmanship.*

Without the development of hand skills, the program offered is not vocational education. This is not to say that other educational programs do not develop hand skills. The difference is in the employment objective—the use to which the skills are to be put.

12. *A quality program provides for the learning of the technology, mathematics, science, drawing, or art related to the occupation.*

This is necessary for success in the occupation and a complete understanding and appreciation of the occupation. The related subjects reinforce and supplement the shop or laboratory work. Each motivates the other.

Realistic Shop Experience

13. *A quality program uses methods, materials, and equipment as similar to actual working conditions as is practical in a school situation, and schedules a sufficient amount of continuous shop or laboratory time to carry through the learning experiences.*

Training takes time and shortcuts short-change the student. The more realistic the shop experience, the easier the transition to employment.

14. *A quality program provides*

for a systematic evaluation of its effectiveness through periodic review, performance tests and written examinations, and follow-up studies of its graduates.

Evaluation is going on all the time in an informal way. Every time an employer hires one of our graduates he will evaluate our program on the basis of how well the worker performs.

In conclusion, a quality program can be operated in a wide variety of educational institutions. The evalu-ative criteria suggested can be applied in any institution and at any grade level. They can be applied to any field or area of vocational education: trade and industrial, distributive, home economics, business and office occupations, technical, agriculture, or health occupations.

If we adhere to these principles, our programs will have the quality and stability to meet the needs of the youth and adults we are dedicated to serve.

Foundations

FOUNDATIONS OF INDUSTRIAL ARTS EDUCATION

By Ronald L. Koble

A basic concern of industrial arts educators, since its emergence as an identifiable entity in the program of the common school during the late nineteenth and early twentieth centuries, has been the precise documentation of its foundations. Lacking the direction that would have been provided by the documentation of its foundations, industrial arts has grown without a comprehensive and generally accepted statement of purpose. What has resulted is the proliferation of a variety of programs that are classified as industrial arts education. A great amount of time and effort have been expended in the past in defining industrial arts and developing lists of goals or objectives, but these efforts did not result in any substantive progress. Collectively, these initial efforts can be viewed as attempts by the profession to clarify its function as an educational program. The literature is replete with definitions, objectives, goals, statements of purpose, and a few program proposals. A primary historical problem in the field of industrial arts has been to discover some agreement among these definitions, objectives, goals and statements of purpose. The problem of obtaining agreement regarding the mission of industrial arts as an integral component of the common school program is attributed by many to the independence afforded the profession in its formative stages because its foundations were not explicitly defined.

In Retrospect

In retrospect, it appears that efforts to identify a logical basis for the existence of industrial arts education as one aspect of the education of all students that have occurred in the past five or six years will be viewed as a "coming of age" period for the field. Very briefly, recent attempts to identify the foundations of industrial arts education can be grouped into several categories which are not mutually exclusive. They are described as follows:

Occupational Oriented - Proponents of this rationale view industrial arts education as an integral part of a program primarily concerned with occupational preparation. Industrial Arts is viewed as one of the stages of a continuous program whose primary focus is on preparation for gainful employment. Another point on this continuum is the secondary school vocational program. Emphasis is placed normally on performance, with special attention given to the development of psychomotor skills.

Industry-Technology Oriented - Proponents of this position support the view that the purpose of education is to transmit and improve the culture, and that an important segment or aspect of the American culture is its distinct technological nature. Thus, a program in the common school intended to familiarize students with technology is needed. Industrial arts education is viewed as a school program that concerns itself with that segment of technology utilized by industry in the production of goods. This program is viewed as a necessary aspect of the liberal or general education of all students.

Technology Oriented - Proponents of this position focus on man as the creator of technology, including its technical as well as its cultural aspects. Viewed as a necessary and important component of the liberal or general education of everyone, it includes a study of the historical, anthropological, social, and economic aspects of the culture . . . man interacting with technology in the culture.

Several important elements can be abstracted from these three statements. First, a most fundamental concern of education is related to familiarizing man with his environment in order to permit him to function at a maximized level of efficiency and effectiveness. Second, one aspect of the education of everyone should pertain to technology, industry or occupations.

Historically, those proponents who view industrial arts as one phase of a total program of occupational preparation have not felt the need to identify the foundations upon which industrial arts is based because they have existed from the time primitive man first taught his offspring how to perform a task. Programs in manual training and manual arts that existed many years ago were deeply rooted in this vocational or occupational orientation. As previously mentioned, industrial arts was justified because of its contribution to the eventual gainful employment of those enrolled in the program. As a result, these programs in the common school usually assume a structure consistent with existing vocational programs.

Isolated efforts to change the focus of industrial arts during the twentieth century by small groups in and out of the field have been made from time to time. Until recently, these efforts were essentially philosophical and were not transmitted into activity programs on a recognizable scale. As a result, the nature of industrial arts today in the United States, as confirmed by recent national studies, remains as it existed when it emerged as a part of the program of the common school, although modest modifications have been made in its orientation, breadth, and methodology.

Current Efforts

Two factors can be attributed to the substantive efforts currently being made to identify the foundations of industrial arts education. One has been mentioned in a prior reference which indicated that the profession was "coming of age." In the developmental period of an emerging entity, there is a period usually when a field must find itself by probing into the unknown. Hopefully, industrial arts has reached the end of this initial period of searching. Another factor closely related to current efforts being made to identify the foundations of industrial arts has been the availability of funds of sufficient magnitude to support major developmental projects. These have been provided primarily by the federal government with some support by private foundations.

To almost everyone, implicit in the identification or development of the foundations of any body of knowledge is the establishment and subsequent recognition of the body of related knowledge as a discipline. When the term discipline is used, it implies (a) the existence of a body of established knowledge, and (b) agreement among specialists in the field on the boundaries of that body of knowledge.

Previously noted were the efforts of the "Industry-Technology Oriented" and "Technology Oriented" movements in industrial arts to recognize industrial arts as a discipline. These efforts are now aimed at identifying the parameters of the body of knowledge for industrial arts which would give the field a meaningful and more prestigous place as an educational program.

A discipline has several distince characteristics:

    (a) The body of knowledge of a discipline is related; it can be structured around major concepts or principles.

(b) The body of knowledge is collective, it has become a body of related knowledge because new knowledge is added through scientific investigation.

(c) The body of knowledge, although unique and identifiable in its own right, is not completely independent of other disciplines. It utilizes the discoveries of other fields to support its own knowledge bases.

(d) The body of knowledge is sufficiently constant to endure, but is modified by the accumulation of new knowledge and the deletion of previously accepted information.

Current efforts to document the foundations of industrial arts can be categorized as either industry-technology oriented or technology oriented. Both of these efforts view education as a means of transmitting and improving the culture. Also common to these efforts is the notion that technology is a very important, dynamic, and influential aspect of the American culture, and that everyone should know something about its influence. At this point the similarity ends. The industry-technology oriented group views industrial arts education as a study of the technology utilized by industry to produce industrial products. The management practices of planning and organizing required to support the production of industrial material products become as important as the actual production of goods in a comprehensive study of technology. The management function of hiring and training of employees required to produce products becomes as important as a study of the tool skills or processes used in actual production. In this sense, industrial arts is viewed as a study of the technology used by industry to produce goods. Acceptance of this broader interpretation of the mission of industrial arts as contrasted with its traditional occupational-orientation results in the necessity of imposing certain restrictions. Industrial arts must not be a study of all industries (banking, entertainment, and financial are excluded, as well as others) but that entity concerned with the production of industrial material products. The foundations of this position include: (a) The American culture is technological, (b) the purpose of education is to transmit and improve the culture, (c) industrial-technology should be understood by everyone, and, therefore, (d) a discipline-based program in the common school is necessary.

The technology-oriented group view technology as a study of the unique means man has devised to function efficiently in the culture. This group would view the study of the influence of technology on man as a primary element and of the same importance as a study of technology itself. The technology developed by man to make his existence more enjoyable and efficient is examined without restriction to industry. Thus, a consideration of the technological elements and cultural implications of a mechanical heart or a device developed to monitor air pollution would be as appropriate to the study of what has been called industrial arts as a comprehensive consideration of the automated production of aluminum containers or automobiles. As previously mentioned, technology would be examined from its anthropological, economic, historical, and social aspects.

The difference between the "Industry-Technology Oriented" position and the "Technology-Oriented" position is modest when compared to the Occupational Oriented position. While the resolution of these differences is important, more significant is the fact that the foundations related to industrial arts education are being identified.

FOUNDATIONS OF INDUSTRIAL EDUCATION

By Everett R. Glazener

Other assignments in this issue of the JOURNAL are concerned both generally and specifically with the topics of Vocational and Practical Arts Education, Trade and Industrial Education, and Industrial Arts. The theme of the issue is to explore the roots of these applied discipline areas and the fourth area (or term) Industrial Education. In one brief article (or several articles) it is not realistic to assume that all of the philosophical, psychological, sociological or economic foundations as they relate to each topic can be developed totally and sufficiently to the satisfaction of any one reader or group. At best, only a brief discussion of relationships and interpretations should be expected in this wide spectrum of subjects and subject areas.

Meanings of the Terms

To what are we referring when we use the above terms, names of programs or disciplines? What is your definition or interpretation of these? Ask any group of professionals in one or all of these educational programs what their understanding is of them and there will be numerous and varied responses and interpretations, some quite unrelated. However, there are direct and indirect relationships between all of them. It is wishful thinking to believe that everyone would agree with one set of definitions and interpretations of names and terms. Nevertheless, in the context of this article, such an explanation is attempted before other relationships are presented. Historical precedence, the influence of tradition, the implications of recent legislation, and the varied use of terms by different groups make such an attempt at clarification a rather difficult task. Experience will prove without a doubt that there is often disagreement, and frequently misunderstanding, of terminology among personnel within these programs. Is it any wonder that the general public is confused?

For a better in-depth study of past history, all personnel in these related fields should read the various education and industrially-related histories, the volumes by Bennett (1926, 1937), and the recent compilation of the history of industrial education in the United States by Barlow (1967) as some examples. It is both surprising and shocking that many teachers within industrial arts, vocational-industrial education, and technical education have neither read even portions of histories nor had other comparable experiences designed to further their understanding of the varied industrial programs.

Vocational Education

Any form of education—formal or informal, practical or theoretical, academic or manipulative skill oriented—could be loosely called vocational education. However, from the historical and traditional standpoint, from early to present legislation, this form of education in America has usually been interpreted to be a form of training at the secondary, post-secondary, and adult educational levels to develop within the individual the knowledges (including practice), habits, and attitudes essential for entry into occupations for which the person is receiving training. This could also include retraining and updating within an occupation. In the past, the most common occupational areas have been those in agriculture, homemaking, and trade and industrial or single craft occupations, such as a carpenter, electrician, machinist, welder, plumber, or brick mason. Examples of later developments would be training in distributive (sales) occupations, building trades, metal trades, business and office education, health occupations, and various technician or technical education occupations.

The recent General Report of the Advisory Council on Vocational Education shows that approximately seven million people were enrolled in the above occupational training areas in 1967. Quoting from this report:

Why is vocational education necessary? It is the bridge between man and his work. Millions of people need this education in order to earn a living. Every man wants to provide for his family with honor and dignity and to be counted as an individual. Providing for an individual's employability as he leaves school, and throughout his worklife, is one of the major goals of vocational education. Vocational education looks at a man as a part of society and as an individual, and never before has attention to the individual as a person been so imperative (1968).

Practical Arts Education

The existence of the practical arts education program within schools does not insinuate that all other education is impractical. The term "practical arts education" is a generic term applied to the several types of functional or general education which is of value to all students. This education usually embraces the study of activities through which natural resources are secured, processed, distributed, and used to meet some physical needs of man. Such activities as general homemaking, general business education, general agriculture, fine arts, and industrial arts would be placed in this category—programs in which occupational or trade efficiency is not a major goal. Manipulative activities may be quite limited or rather extensive.

Trade and Industrial Education

Reference to this term by different individuals may take on various meanings. Possibly one of the best comprehensive names would be Vocational-Industrial Education. One of the most frequently used names is the abbreviated form of T. & I. Examples of particular types of training in this vocational education program are diversified occupations (D.O.), commonly called Industrial Cooperative Training (I.C.T.) in some areas, apprenticeship training, and the skilled craft occupational groupings. These programs are for entry into and progress in the occupations related thereto, especially oriented to trades, industry, and manufacturing.

Industrial Arts

Industrial arts is a program usually taught in the secondary schools, but it may be found at all levels of some schools from kindergarten through the twelfth grade. The real intent of such a program is to be education of a general nature for any student and should provide learning experiences to give insight into and orientation about the industrial and technological world in which we live. Industrial arts, as a general rule, should not be for the purpose of preparing students for specific occupational employment, any more so than other general education or so-called academic subjects. Although many disagree, it can be used in a guidance and prevocational function for some students and even directed toward vocational use in limited situations. The largest criticism usually directed toward this program in the schools today is that the industrial and technical orientation is far too limited and outdated and that too many programs direct their attention to manipulative skill development with little or no relationships being made to exemplify industry and technological developments in securing raw products, development, production and distribution of goods.

Industrial Education

In the broad sense of explaining this term, it might be stated that any education related to industry could be called industrial education. It should not be considered a specific program but a general term referring to most or all programs which are industrially-oriented and more particularly have been considered in a traditional sense as manipulative in nature. Historically and up to recent years the term has been used to refer to a group of programs including Vocational-Industrial Education (Trade and Industrial Education or T. & I.), Industrial Arts, and more recently Technical Education. There are those who use the term Industrial Education to refer to a specific vocational program, but this use would be discouraged.

As history has recorded, the above programs have evolved from early indentured apprenticeship, and from European and Russian developments related to both general education and early engineering education. Compared to the age of academic education, public free education, and similar developments in formal education, these programs of training in the secondary schools and colleges are relatively new. Manual training and manual arts were also terms evolved in earlier years in a period of history when manipulative learning was most needed in individual programs. In the earlier developmental years, the types of industrial education being taught at different levels were a kind of general use education for some and for others had objectives of occupational training. No clear-cut distinction was really evident, and it is probable that there are programs still in operation where such distinction cannot be made.

When the vocational education act was enacted (Smith-Hughes Act of 1917), this legislation was considered by many to have given a clear division or separation of the general or practical arts programs from the occupational or vocational education programs of which industrial arts and vocational-industrial education are parts, respectively. Some are quick to add that these two programs have become parallel, component parts of education, related in many ways, and contribute to the support of each other. Many unfortunate disagreements regarding this relationship continue to our present time.

These two industrial education programs have developed largely at the secondary school level. Relatively few college and university programs in this area of activity were developed before the enactment of the 1917 law. As the secondary programs developed and expanded, to a great extent because of federal support, a need arose for properly prepared teachers. With few exceptions, the Federal Land-Grant Colleges and Universities developed programs and curricula for certifying vocational-industrial teachers and either later or simultaneously developed a program for industrial arts teachers. The normal school, or later teachers colleges and universities, also developed departments and curricula largely for preparing industrial arts teachers. Many of the departments were multi-purpose in objectives and curricula.

Since the term industrial education had been used for many years and had evolved as a multi-purpose term, it is probable that a large number of post-secondary departments and programs assumed this name or title to designate this work. By the middle 1950's at least thirty-five different names could be found for departmental titles with a large number using "industrial education" in some way. Possibly it is safe to assume without a factual survey that the term industrial education was and still is in considerable use to designate departments which prepare predominantly vocational-industrial education and industrial arts teachers.

However, technical education and all of the ramifications of technology and the atomic space age have brought about additional needs for training workers and teachers. Technical education, especially as it relates to industry and manufacturing, is now being included by many departments under the umbrella term Industrial Education. Two-year programs in special schools, in junior or community colleges, and in some universities, as well as four-year degree programs have developed and are evolving for both the preparation of workers and a few for specific technical teacher preparation.

A brief survey of the *Industrial Teacher Education Directory* for 1968-69, cooperatively sponsored by the ACIATE and the NAITTE, will show a predominance of the terms industrial education and industrial arts as parts of departmental names. It will also be found that Technology has been added to numerous titles or that colleges and divisions have been established in many higher education institutions with separate departments for the various industrial education curricula. Some colleges and universities continue to operate the various curricula in one Department of Industrial Education, where more than one option is available. Two or more such options in one department may be those of industrial arts teacher education, vocational-industrial teacher education, non-teaching options that are basically structured as industrial arts, technical teacher education, industrial technology, industrial management, industrial distribution, and engineering technology.

It is doubtful that the problem if a problem actually exists in local situations, will be settled in the near future, if ever. Yet there are many discussions developing centered on the subject of whether various options should be offered and if teachers and others should be educated in the same department. Some pros and cons of this issue have been presented in the winter 1967 issue of the *Journal of Industrial Teacher Education*.

REFERENCES

Advisory Council on Vocational Education. *Vocational Education: The Bridge Between Man and His Work*. General Report of the Advisory Council on Vocational Education to the U.S. Dept. of H.E.W. Washington, D.C.: Govt. Printing Office, 1968.

Barlow, M. *History of Industrial Education in the United States*. Peoria, Ill.: C.A. Bennett, 1967.

Bennett, C.A. *History of Manual and Industrial Education Up to 1870*. Peoria, Ill.: C.A. Bennett, 1926.

Bennett, C.A. *History of Manual and Industrial Education, 1870 to 1917*. Peoria, Ill.: C.A. Bennett, 1937.

THE FUNCTION & STRUCTURE OF INDUSTRIAL ARTS IN THE EDUCATIONAL PHILOSOPHY OF ALFRED NORTH WHITEHEAD

by

M. James Bensen

INTRODUCTION

In view of the fact that Alfred North Whitehead is one of the most original and imaginative of twentieth century philosophers, his views on education are of special interest. Both his general philosophy and his writings on education are provocative, fresh, and full of suggestions for action.[1]

A few contemporary thinkers subscribe to the extravagant claim that Whitehead is the greatest philosopher of all time. Even though this claim may be extreme, no one I am certain, would deny that he made a deep impression on contemporary philosophy.[2]

The curriculum of the American high school and college has been under heavy pressures of expansion such as Whitehead probably never dreamed of at the time he wrote about education. As these "new" courses press for a place in the curriculum, provisions need to be made to fit them into the total structure of his theoretical system.

Industrial arts education is one of the areas that has developed since this period and is now playing an important role in the school curriculum. An attempt is made here to analyze the educational philosophy of Whitehead as it is presented in his writings (as well as those who write about him) and then determine the function and the structure of industrial arts within the theory he proposes. A few graphical illustrations are introduced that represent some of Whitehead's ideas as conceptualized by this writer. Other illustrations are introduced to better portray the function and structure of industrial arts education within Whitehead's educational system.

WHITEHEAD'S EDUCATIONAL PHILOSOPHY

Introduction

Alfred North Whitehead has been long renowned for his work in logic, mathematics, and general philosophy, but it is only recently that his writing in the field of education has begun to receive a great deal of readership and popularity. The basic cause of the interest in Whitehead's essays seem to lie in the fact that they are gems of perceptiveness, moral earnestness, and wit.[3]

The Purpose of Education

Schools should contribute to the education and development of the individual as a whole, therefore, the purpose of education according to Whitehead is to give the individual a general as well as a special education. Whitehead apparently recognized no conflict in an education which includes both technological and liberal educational aspects, as he pointed out specifically that "schools should attend to the ballanced development of both aesthetic and intellectual aspects of education."[4]

The two great principles of conservatism and progressivism should be maintained in a balanced state. Wegener refers to this as being "bipolar" and that it is complementary to a dynamic society.[5] Industrial arts, as a part of general education, must make its contribution to the balanced education of each student by providing him with the knowledge, skills, and attitudes of our technological culture.

The Purpose of Teachers

Teachers within the Whitehead system of education have two main obligations or roles to fulfill in aiding the students to learn.[6] The first function of a teacher is to prevent waste by pruning out "unessential stuff" from the material that students study. This calls for a continuous process of curriculum study and revision. This is especially true in our present space age culture where knowledge is exploding and time becomes an extremely important variable. The second function of teachers is to elicit enthusiasm from the student and thus establish a firmer purpose to learning. Motivation is extremely important for Whitehead points out that 'education above all should be 'enjoyable' to the student."[7]

The industrial arts teacher in Whitehead's system of education would be a stimulating and motivating "facilitator of learning." His function would be to guide his students toward excellence in their creative efforts. There would be a careful blending of the technological principles as the teacher utilizes the problem-solving approach in the laboratory setting.

Active Learners

It is important that students are allowed to examine their views and actively participate in the learning process. Problem-solving techniques and creativity are essential and must replace the mere memorization of facts and figures. The surge of creativity in the learning process is the motive power and the ultimate source of educational growth. "The formal processes of education are one complex means by which the creative advance into novelty is, in the case of mankind, rendered more efficient and more fruitful."[8]

Learners are responsible for their own "acquiring of knowledge" through active mental and physical participation. The role of the teacher is to aid this learning process by careful and constant curriculum revision and by presenting a stimulating learning climate that arouses enthusiasm in the student. The industrial arts laboratory would be utilized to its fullest extent, in presenting an "action" setting, which would foster as much active participation on the part learners as deemed feasible.

THE CYCLIC THEORY

An Overview of the Concept

Whitehead's rhythmic cycle theory draws some of its elements from the earlier philosophic reflections of Hegel. When Hegel analyzed progress into three stages, which he called Thesis, Anthesis, and Synthesis, Whitehead concluded that these terms were not suggestive enough for his purpose of applying this idea to educational theory.[9]

In relation to Hegel's analysis, Whitehead identifies these periods in his dynamic theory of the "rhythmic cycle." In this theory he refers to these three states as the stage of Romance, the stage of Precision, and the stage of Generalization.

ILLUSTRATION OF THE THREE STAGES
OF A "RHYTHMIC CYCLE"

Whitehead points out in his essays that life itself is essentially periodic and is composed of well-marked yearly periods.[10] Thus, man is subject to these cycles in all aspects of his development, whether they occur physically, mentally, during his formal education, or even life itself.

The term "rhythm" is introduced to the cycle theory to identify a type of re-cycling phenomona that greatly influences our lives. In these cyclic recurrences the subordinate stages are reproduced in each cycle yet the gross or subtler periods are always different as we pass from cycle to cycle. Whitehead uses the term "rhythmic" as meaning essentially the conveyance of difference within the framework of repetition.[11]

The Romance Stage

The romance period or stage always occurs first in the cycle and it is the period of first apprehension. There can be no mental development without interest and the romantic stage provides this in the educational cycle. A typical reaction on the part of the individual during this romance period are those of discovery, allurement, immediate joys, arousement, and incitement of pleasureable activity. During this period learning and concept formation take place in a haphazard way as there are vague apprehensions of unlimited broad generalities. These are almost always acquired in a zestful and unsophisticated manner.

The learner displays characteristics of being selfmotivating as emotion and excitement tend to lure him toward the unexplored territory that lies just ahead in the "precision state." As a result, knowledge acquired during the romantic stage is not dominated by systematic procedure.[12]

The Precision Stage

The "precision" period of the cycle follows the romatic stage. It represents also an addition to knowledge, but it is evident that the systematic and exactness of the conditions under which this knowledge is acquired would be barren without a previous stage of romance.[13]

Here in the precision stage an analysis of the previously acquired generalization takes place along with the acquisition of other facts. This acquisition of new knowledge is gained in a systematic order thereby disclosing ideas with possibilities of a wide significance.

The Generalization Stage

The final stage in the rhythmic cycle is called the "generalization" period. It is a return to romanticism with the newly gained advantage of classified ideas and relevant techniques and thought.[14] It is the fruition which has been the goal of the precision training. The generalization stage therefore allows one to reach into our store of experience and training and draw out workable solutions to problems that confront us.

Implications for Education and Life

When examining the structure of the cyclic theory it is noted that the three stages must occur in sequential order. Whitehead states however that there is no point where one stage ceases and another begins. He points that there is, however, a period where one becomes strongly dominant and the others tend to take on support roles. The example that is illustrated shows how the period of romance, though dominant in the first stage, is still present in the latter two stages and likewise the precision and generalization stages operate in the same manner.

The life of an individual is a constant growth and rhythm of such pulsating cycles. Some of these cycles are small and take a very short time to complete; but they may in turn serve as a romance stage for some larger cycle.[15]

GRAPHIC ILLUSTRATION OF A RHYTHMIC CYCLE
WITH EMPHASIS ON THE DOMINANT
SEQUENTIAL STAGES

Life itself could be visualized as a "grand cycle" which is made up of all the lesser cycles experienced by the individual which are acting in support roles as they are interwoven together. It should be recalled that each cycle whether it is large or small, is made up of the romance, precision, and generalization stages. A graphic sketch attempts to relate how a few cycles can relate themselves to each other in many different ways.

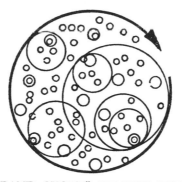

THE "GRAND CYCLE"—ILLUSTRATING THE
SUPPORTING & INTER-WOVEN CYCLES

The rhythm of education does not subscribe to the theory that easier subjects should be taught before the harder. On the contrary, some of the hardest must come first as many life tasks do because they are essential to life. Whitehead illustrates this in the following way.

The first intellectual task that confronts an infant is the acquirement of a spoken language. What an appaling task, the correlation of meanings and sounds! We all know that the infant does it, and the miracle of his achievement is explicable.[16]

It should be acknowledged that the education cycle for each individual will differ from all others. The stages that Whitehead proposes are general as to the year the individuals enter and leave these stages as the dominant force in their educational cycle. This cycle begins in the elementary school which is the starting place of the romantic stage in the larger educational cycle. This period of romance is of course made up of smaller complete cycles and this stage continues on until about age thirteen or fourteen, which corresponds to about the last year in junior high school.

In the ninth or tenth grade the student enters into the precision stage and this is dominant until about the age of eighteen or when most students finish high school. The generalization stage dominates the educational cycle until about age twenty-two for all practical purposes. This stage then corresponds to the age when students are in college, learning skills in trade school, or entering their first full-time job.

It becomes apparent that some people never really fit this pattern due to lack of motivation or hyper-acceleration and numerous other reasons. Within this general educational cycle it is pointed out by Whitehead that different courses in the curriculum reach their dominant stages at widely varied ages in youth. As an illustration of this; language is in the precision stage during junior high school while science is just in the romance period at this time.[17]

The Structure of Industrial Arts Within the Cyclic Theory

To visualize the structure of industrial arts within the framework of the cyclic theory, an analysis has to be made of some of shorter cycles which are eddying forth, overlapping and recurring, but each consisting of the same rhythmic pattern of romance, precision, and generalization.

The first problem that is solved or the project that is constructed in an industrial arts laboratory may be thought of as a small but complete cycle.[18] The student becomes pleasantly excited as well as a little apprehensive in the early stages of shaping his thoughts and ideas that will have an influence on his project. When this condition is present he is in the stage of romance. The good smell of fresh wood chips, the action of the class in handling of the tools and materials, as well as the planned motivational activities of the teacher all have a direct bearing on the strength of the romance stage which will in turn have much effect on the student's performance in the later stages of the cycle.

The precision stage in the individual project becomes dominant as the student systematically studies the designing, planning, and technological principles that must be incorporated into the project plan. The precision stage is further developed as he works with the materials in the actual construction of the project. A wealth of information is collected and classified as the project progressed through its operations. A good deal of this information comes from the teacher, but much is discovered by the student himself as he applies problem solving methods to arrive at satisfactory solutions.

The stage of generalization, as stated earlier, is a return to the stage of romance, thereby completing the three-fold cycle. The return is with additional knowledge, classified ideas, and techniques to augment and broaden the original concepts. The generalization stage becomes dominant in the project as the student nears its completion. He can now draw upon his acquired knowledge which was gained from the two earlier stages and use this in decision-making and value judgments. He may view his project much more critically now and will take mental notes on how to correct his mistakes in future activities. As he is completing the first project new thoughts and ideas are being formed in this generalization stage that will provide the fuel for the romance stage that will follow (in the second problem or project, etc.) as exposure to new activities are becoming apparent to him.

We can see then that each cycle builds, supports and interlocks with future cycles which become more sophisticated and higher level as the student moves through a spiral or hierarchy of activities. In addition to the project other "short" or supporting cycles are evident in industrial arts. A visit to an industrial plant, working on a technical report, informal observation of a complex operation being performed by an advanced student, and discovering solutions to problem-solving activities are some examples.

The romance stage of the "grand cycle of industrial arts" evidently starts taking on a dominant theme somewhere in the upper grades of elementary school. This is where boys take on a strong desire for handling tools, and gain some experience in "dad's workshop," as well as through construction and craft activities in scouting.

This stage of the cycle continues and grows in its dominance as the student enters junior high school. The new industrial arts student finds himself in an exploratory type of program which is especially designed to exploit this stage of romance. He finds one unit more exciting than the last and at the end of his adventure of exploring industry in the laboratory he finds it difficult to make a decision as to his preference of the units that were taught.

The precision stage takes on the dominant force at about grade nine or ten. Usually the exploratory type of course gives away to a more structured and specific unit of study. The courses in grades nine and ten are in most cases the second time that the student has experienced working in the particular medium. The contents of these courses require the student to search, discover, and categorize a wide range of technical and cultural information that he will apply in the laboratory sessions.

The generalization stage in the grand cycle of industrial arts becomes dominant in the last year or two of high school and it continues on after he has graduated from high school. At this point in the cycle the student returns to the romantic stage with all the advantages that he gained from the previous stages.

It should be remembered that this "grand cycle" is not rigid and the different stages may vary considerably from one individual to another. It becomes apparent that the more students that we bring to the generalization stage in industrial arts before they graduate from high school, the greater the opportunity they will have to utilize the contributions of their earlier industrial arts experiences.

THE STRUCTURE OF MAJOR EDUCATIONAL CURRICULUMS

Major Curriculums

Education under Whitehead's system takes on three major forms or curriculums. Since each individual has his own special needs and the time element dictates that he can not study all fields in depth, the curriculums are divided into the literary, scientific and the technical fields. Once the major curriculums have been established, Whitehead warns against making any "fatal disconnections" between the subjects. . ." you may not divide the seamless cloak of learning. There is only one subject matter for education and that is life in all its manifestations."[19]

GRAPHIC ILLUSTRATION OF THE THREE
MAJOR CURRICULUMS

What must be sought out is a synthesis such that these curriculums include the other two and that each should be illuminated by the others. In order to make these three curriculums function effectively a careful co-ordination of the basic elements must be made. Because of the lack of time the emphasis must be on the specific individual curriculums with the teaching of related principles and generalities that are synthesized from the other two supplemental bodies of knowledge.

Every form of education should give the pupil a technique, a science, an assortment of general ideas, and aesthetic appreciation.[20]

The Function of Industrial Arts Within the Curriculum

The function of industrial arts lends itself particularly well to the structure of the technical curriculum. Whitehead states that the technical curriculum should not become too specialized but must include creativity, logic of discovery (problem-solving?), and experiences which teach you to co-ordinate act and thought. This experience leads one to associate thought with foresight and foresight with achievement. Technical education gives theory, and a shrewd insight as to where insight fails.[21]

Due to the specifications that Whitehead outlines as the essential elements of the technical curriculum, industrial arts is ideally introduced into all three curriculum structures through the technical portion.

THE PLACE OF INDUSTRIAL ARTS IN THE
TECHNICAL EDUCATION CURRICULUM

In the scientific and literary curriculums industrial arts would still effectively function within the realm of the technical curriculum. Its purpose within these structures would possibly be to play a greater role in representing the technical aspect in the curriculum.

Whitehead has specifically stated that these three major curriculums are to be carefully synthesized with each other so that they become integrated and functional.

A CONCLUDING STATEMENT

Industrial arts in its present state is an elective course in most senior high schools, consequently many of the college bound students are not electing these courses in order to meet the entrance requirements which stipulate the scheduling of mostly "hard core" subjects. This situation forces students to leave the "grand cycle" of industrial arts in many different stages of development. A great number of students have no development past the romance stage in industrial arts experiences.

One of the chief concerns of every industrial arts teacher should be carrying out the responsibility of giving each student a balanced education. In a society where much emphasis is put on seeking a college education, an over-balance is put on the stress of scientific and literary curriculums and less interest is shown in the technical areas. Progressive industrial arts programs can fulfill the needs of putting this education back into balance for all students.

Industrial arts, as an important part of any curriculum, would have to justify itself as a dynamic and contributing area of study or Whitehead would not endorse it in the total school program. To avoid the violation of Whitehead's two "educational commandments," (teach fewer things and teach them well) the contemporary industrial arts program must put emphasis on: 1) stimulating creativity, 2) teach by the problem solving method, 3) address itself to real issues in industry and technology (prune out the "inert" ideas), and 4) occasionally integrate with other courses by giving students first hand experience in making practical applications in research and development.

REFERENCES

Burnett, Joe R. "Alfred North Whitehead," *Educational Theory*, Vol. 11, (October, 1961), (Footnotes # 3, 7).

Dunkle, Harold B. *Whitehead on Education*, Columbus, Ohio: The Ohio State University Press, 1965. (# 1, 7, 8).

Harford, Edward J. "The Rhythm of Learning and the Project," *School Shop*, Vol. 23, (December, 1963), (# 18).

Lowe, Victor, Hartshorene, Charles, and Johnson, A. H. (Preface by A. C. Benjamin), *Whitehead and the Modern World*, Boston: The Beacon Press, 1950. (# 2).

Wegener, Frank C. "Alfred North Whitehead: An Implied Philosophy of School and Society," *Educational Theory*, Vol 11 (October, 1961), (#4, 5).

Whitehead, Alfred North, *The Aims of Education*, New York: The MacMillan Co., 1929, (#9, 10, 11, 12, 13, 14, 15, 16, 17, 19, 20, 21).

INDUSTRY AIDS EDUCATION

by Ronald W. Stadt

Journalists, representatives of labor, lay groups, and educators often suggest that industry should assume greater responsibility for education. Many people who voice this opinion follow a whoever-spills-the milk-mops-it-up kind of policy. When confronted with accelerating technological change and commensurate demands for education and expertise, many people are quick to submit that industry is the major cause of educational lag and that industry should therefore shoulder major responsibility for reducing educational lag. Some people follow general statements with specific recommendations—often in the fashion of sidewalk superintendents. Some industrialists agree, at least in part, with this thinking, but some are equally quick to submit that it is nonsense to expect the fellow who lets the cat out of the bag to put it back.

The purpose of this article is not to debate this issue or to establish guidelines for determining industry's projected role in education. Rather the purpose of this article is to present some facts the reader should consider before coming to grips with the issue.

Before one can adopt a position regarding the kind and degree of responsibilities industry should accept because of the technological privileges it exercises, he should become familiar with the nature of industry's present educational efforts. Industry's educational efforts can be grouped into two reasonable discreet categories: (1) education within industry, and (b) aid to education outside industry.

The kind of description of education within industry which could be given here would be quite sketchy and would not add to the industrial educator's present understanding. Industry conducts endless varieties of educational programs and vocational educators have become reasonably familiar with them. A general treatment of the subject being rather meaningless, this article will be devoted to a discussion of industry aid to education.

Gifts and other forms of aid have long augmented the educator's budget. Industry has a long history of friendly and helpful relations with other institutions, and educators, especially, have long since come to welcome contributions, grants-in-aid, special privileges and other forms of assistance from industry. Since 1950, industry has quadrupled expenditures for aid to education and is now spending more than two hundred million dollars per year.

REASONS FOR AID

Companies have a diversity of reasons for aiding education. Some companies contribute without carefully analyzing their reasons, but increasing numbers give aid according to carefully designed plans which yield maximum short and/or long-term returns. Some of the major reasons for aid to education are obvious.

Improved Manpower Resource

Many companies assist educational agencies to foster direct or indirect improvements in their manpower supply. School bond issues not excluded, progressive firms are happy to promote public and private educational agencies which contribute either to the level of primary abilities or the level of specific saleable skills in the community. Companies are happy to foster general improvements in education because they then have an improved base on which to develop expertise, and they are happy to foster improvements in special education if they, in turn, need to conduct fewer specialized training programs in the company.

Good Will

Good will is a nebulous commodity but companies do a great deal to foster an image which is compatible with community values. Companies publicize their efforts so that the public as well as students who benefit directly will attach desired values to the company. Companies want it known that they consider education to be very important and go to great lengths at local, national and even international levels to demonstrate their support, knowing full well that increased good will ultimately means improved sales and other benefits for the company and the community.

Income and Consumption

Economists have demonstrated that schooling, income, and consumption are highly correlated. The longer one goes to school, the greater his income, the greater his consumption, the more effort and money he devotes to continuing education. Industry knows it cannot sell ever-more sophisticated products at ever increasing rates if greater numbers of people do not go to school for longer and longer periods before earning larger and larger incomes.

Research

Although a great deal of the monies industry contributes to universities and other non-profit research agencies is not earmarked for products which have direct implications for the sponsoring company, nearly all research benefits one or more industry. The time lag between discovery and application grows ever smaller and the alliance between universities and industry grows ever stronger. Moreover the kinds of research findings which industry utilizes get more and more diverse. Witness the speed with which industry utilizes findings in the behavioral sciences in advertising, market analysis and education.

Company and Brand Name Familiarity

Consumer goods manufacturers go to great lengths to display their products such that brands and labels are impressed upon the young. Some companies supply expensive items such as appliances for home economics laboratories. Many companies offer reading materials, such as company histories with names and pictures of their products generously distributed through the pages. Aid of this kind may result in better sales of the company's products and services or even better sales of its stocks and bonds.

Perpetuation

Many of the materials distributed by industrial and commercial organizations contain arguments in support of free enterprise and against government control. Industry's efforts are often quite indirect but pointed nevertheless. Companies faced with stringent governmental controls and inspections or companies whose competitors are asking for increased government subsidies or tax exemptions, e.g., trucking and railroads, welcome the opportunity to impress the young with the values of the free enterprise system—and this opportunity should not be denied.

Scholarships and Loans

This is probably the fastest growing category of aid. Guidance counselors are equipped with encyclopedic lists of scholarships of numerous kinds. Industry scholarships vary tremendously. Some require students to work for the sponsoring firm for a minimum number of years; many do not. Some require recipients to major in a specific field or to enroll in a given university. Some make very specific requirements regarding grade point average and other indexes of success.

Length varies from one year (usually the senior year) to eight or nine or an unlimited number of years. Probably the largest and least restrictive scholarship is one which makes no requirement regarding major field or institution attended, pays an initial stipend of several thousand dollars during the freshman year, and increases until the stipend in the final year of graduate school is larger than the young PhD. might receive for his first year of full-time work.

Teaching Aids

This category of aid is probably the most diverse. The content and methods of presentation vary greatly. Books, pamphlets, recordings, films and filmstrips, models and working models, museum exhibits, traveling exhibits, samples of product in process, demonstrators and sundry other types of aids are used in almost every kind of educational institution, classroom or laboratory. Many aids are prepared by competent teams of educators and psychologists, employed by industry. Not enough are utilized as effectively as they might be.

Material and Equipment

Many firms donate materials to university research departments and high school laboratories. Chemicals and minerals used in agricultural research or building materials for high school science projects; new or used laboratory or production machines and equipment for research, demonstration, or training purposes; new engines for automotive classes, and, occasionally, an entire laboratory, department, or wing for a vocational school are among the many donations and loans made to public and private educational institutions.

Grants and Gifts

Although it is not unusual for a single firm or an association of companies to contribute an entire building or a sizeable piece of land to a university, more frequently grants are made to the scholarship, research, or occasionally the capital funds of universities, colleges, and institutes. Some grants are made to establish professorships in memory of revered industrialists and or foster study in an area which is of interest to the contributing firm. Gifts are of many kinds, the more common being works of art, libraries, and monies which are earmarked for special projects such as recreational facilities and uniforms for athletic and music groups.

Manpower

Industrialists donate a great deal of free time and effort to education. Some corporations have men who devote the major part of their time to consulting with educators and speaking before student groups at graduations, career days, and other special events. Many manhours are contributed by advisory committee members, plant guides, guest lecturers, resource people on television documentaries, and others who are asked to serve the ends of educational institutions. Infrequently, but increasingly, companies donate a year or more of a man's time to educational and research projects conducted by universities, the military or governmental agencies.

Miscellaneous

Several additional educational activities of large corporations deserve mention. Companies support a lot of non-profit organizations such as trade associations which publish free pamphlets and films and engage in other educational activities of value to the general public. They also sponsor educational television and radio programs—often without commercials. Companies cooperate with many schools to conduct work-study programs for business and distributive or diversified occupations for students. Large firms have also conducted teacher-study programs of many types and several have offered special seminars and conferences for school administrators. New developments in the technology of education and instruction on how to use new machines to achieve established general educational purposes are by no means the least valuable of the many aids which industry contributes to contemporary education.

SUMMARY

Although many laymen and some educators would assign increased responsibility for education to the corporations that raise the criteria for expertise, it is evident that many companies conduct internal educational programs and make voluntary contributions to education outside industry. The fact that industry has greatly increased the kinds, frequency, and dollar costs of aid in recent years, should be carefully weighed by those who would increase corporate taxes or increase industry's participation in the educational enterprise by any means. Education is rapidly becoming the major activity of progressive societies and the specific responsibilities of each of the major institutions—family, church, school, corporation, government—will be increasingly difficult to define.

THE USE OF CENSUS DATA FOR THE IMPLEMENATION OF VOCATIONAL-TECHNICAL EDUCATION PROGRAMS

by

Elmer Kuntz

INTRODUCTION

Are you a Census data user? You probably are if you need:

To plan school districts

To plan and locate area vocational schools, technical institutes and community colleges

To define urban renewal programs

To analyze future expenditures and revenues

To allocate future recreational lands

To develop transportation systems

To determine legislative or county districts

To plan Vocational Programs

To analyze vital statistics

To describe economically depressed areas

To formulate economic development programs

Most State Departments of Education have been looking for reliable sources of information from which to plan and develop one-year, five-year, or ten-year plans for vocational education as prescribed under the Vocational Amendments of 1968.

The Vocational Education Amendments of 1968, Public Law 90-576, "provides that policies and procedures be set forth by the States in the distribution of Federal funds to local educational agencies in the States which policies and procedures shall give due consideration to a number of specific factors."

Generally, these specific factors or criteria used by most states for the implementation of new programs and distribution of monies were as follows:

1. Manpower needs and job opportunities
2. Rate of unemployment compared to state average
3. Percent of unemployment that are youth compared to state average
4. Number of children from low-income families per thousand compared to state average
5. Local agency's wealth per student compared to state average

102

6. Local agency's per pupil cost of education compared to state average

Today, we have a tool for vocational planning that is more reliable than ever before, and that is the 1970 census. Census information indicates the types of occupations presently existing in the community, area, or state, and the volume of workers currently employed in each occupation. These data are vital when planning or modifying occupational programs, since they provide an indication of the availability and possible volume of potential job opportunities.

The census is unique because it reaches into every part of the country and involves, to varying degrees, every person and/or household. In the process of gathering population counts, characteristics, income, and housing information on a national basis at one point in time, statistics are developed that are in direct relationship to each other in terms of comparative values and geographic areas. By its nature, the national census is one of the most versatile tools for analysis of population and housing characteristics.

The 1970 census will prove to be more beneficial than any one of the previous censuses by making available summary computer tapes from which data can be assessed in forms more diverse and useful than can be provided from the traditional printed reports. The statistical results will be available for the country as a whole, for each state, each of more than 3,000 counties, each of more than 20,000 municipalities, and the numerous subdivisions of counties.

CENSUS DATA FOR VOCATIONAL PLANNING

Much information in the 1970 census was included specifically for educational planning at both the state and local level. Two forms of the education data are:

(1) Those which are directed specifically to education (e.g., enrollment in school, level of education completed).

(2) Those which are related indirectly to education (e.g., the socio-economic characteristics of the population).

Subject items from the 1970 census which bear directly on education including the following:

(1) Enrollment Status—ascertained for persons three years and older, who are classified as enrolled in school if they attended regular school or college at any time since February, 1970.

(2) Type of School in Which Enrolled—persons enrolled in school are classified by type of school in terms of public vs. private.

(3) Years of School Completed—ascertained for persons three years of age and over who are asked the highest grade or year of regular school they ever attended up to six or more years of college.

(4) Vocational Training—ascertained for persons 14 years or over who are asked whether they ever completed a vocational training program and who are asked to indicate the main field of such training.

Subject items from the 1970 census which bear indirectly on education include the following:

(1) Demographic Data—age, sex, race, marital status, family relationship, and cross tabulations of these data.
(2) Socio-economic Data—employment status, occupation, type of industry, income and sources of income, disability status, veterans status, and tabulations of these data.

In addition, the results of other censuses are also useful and should be used for vocational planning.

(1) Census of Agriculture—conducted every five years in years ending in four and nine; provides a count of farms, and inventory of agricultural land and the way it is used, the amount of each farm product produced and sold, and inventory of the kinds and numbers of livestock and poultry on farms, information on important farm machines and facilities, a count of people working on farms, and a record of important cash expenditures made by farmers.

(2) Census of Construction—conducted every five years in years ending in two and seven; includes data by kind of business and geography on number of construction establishments, employment, payrolls, payments to sub-contractors, payments for materials, components, supplies, machine rental, and capital expenditures.

(3) Census of Business—conducted every five years in years ending in two and seven; covers number of business establishments, sales or receipts, employees, and payrolls for each kind of retail store and wholesale establishment, and for selected service trades.

(4) Census of Governments—conducted every five years in years ending in two and seven; deals mainly with governmental structure, taxable property values, public employment and governmental finances (broken down into 25 different functions, including education).

(5) Censuses of Manufacturing, Mineral Industries and Commercial Fisheries—conducted every five years at infrequent intervals; provides data on employment and payroll, capital expenditures, inventories, value added, products shipped, cost of fuels and energy, operating costs, and operating characteristics.

(6) Censuses of Transportation—conducted every five years in years ending in two and seven; a series of surveys which provides data on personal travel, use of trucks and shipment of commodities.

The 1970 census will provide more effective and efficient data than ever before in our history—it's up to us to use these data to the best advantage.

PROCEDURE

A survey questionnaire was developed and forwarded to the 50 State Departments of Education requesting responses to the ways that census data was used by the departments for the implementing of Vocational-Technical Education programs in their state. Only 33 (66 percent) of the states returned the questionnaires. The information sought by the questionnaire was as follows:

(1) Does your state use census data to develop the state plan?
(2) Does your state use census data to determine manpower needs as related to implementing vocational-technical occupational training?
(3) Does your state use census data to determine job opportunities as related to placement of graduates from vocational-technical occupational programs?
(4) Does your state use census data for program and/or curriculum development in technical institutes and two-year comprehensive colleges?

Table 1 reveals the results of the survey based upon only the replies of 33 states.

TABLE I
USE MADE OF CENSUS DATA BY STATES

	Yes	Percent	No	Percent
Number of States that use Census Data	26	78	7	22
Number of States that use Census Data to develop State Plans	16	48	17	52
Number of States that use Census Data to determine Manpower Needs	15	45	18	55
Number of States that use Census Data for Program Development	14	42	19	58
Number of States that use Census Data to determine job opportunities	8	24	25	76
Number of States that use Census Data to locate Area Vocational Technical Schools and Colleges	4	12	29	88

CONCLUSIONS

Only 26 of the 33 state departments of education indicated that they use census data.

Seventeen of the states indicated that census data was not used in the development of the State Plan for Vocational-Technical Occupational Education.

Only 15 of the states responding used census data to determine manpower needs as related to planning training programs.

The other items in the table indicate that many of the states do not use census data in such things as determining job opportunities and locations of training centers.

SUMMARY

The information obtained by the survey indicates that much beneficial information secured through the census is not being used to assist in implementing vocational-technical occupational programs in many states.

Many reasons were given as to why census data were not used. Several of the reasons were as follows:

(1) Several states were skeptical of the accuracy of the information collected.
(2) That the information collected has a two to five year lag with poor updating.
(3) There doesn't seem to be a satisfactory method for matching the "occupational groupings" used by the Census Bureau and the Occupational Classifications presented by the Department of Labor in its *Dictionary of Occupational Titles.*
(4) Employment Security Agencies' information seem to be more useful.

Those states that did use census data used the information in planning career (vocational-technical) occupational programs at the local, area, and statewide level.

The most extensive use of direct and indirect census data occurs in the development and preparation of state plans for vocational-technical occupational education.

CONCLUSIONS

In spite of the criticism and arguments against using census data for the implementation of vocational-technical education programs, occupational needs information, at a level of detail heretofore unavailable to educational planners, is one of the direct results of the 1970 census.

The information on population trend data alone, which is a comparison by county and by even smaller census tracts, should reveal any significant shifts in population concentrations. Service to the populace can be planned according:

for example, ethnic data can be used to plan service for those disadvantaged by race.

The income data can provide a valuable source of information to be used in planning programs and services for the economically disadvantaged. Employment data from the 1970 census may be used in planning programs to more accurately meet the needs of a given service area. Such information could be used to budget short-term courses according to the needs indicated by employment data and population concentrations.

Generally speaking, never has such information been available for use in planning vocational-technical programs as is represented in the 1970 census. The advantages of its availability far out-weigh the disadvantages suggested in the summary section.

BASIC BELIEFS

IN

DISTRIBUTIVE EDUCATION

Lucy C. Crawford

A PHILOSOPHY of distributive education is but a part of larger and more inclusive philosophies. As pointed out by Orin B. Graff and Calvin M. Street in their work, *Improving Competence in Educational Administration*, a philosophy of education and any of its subdivisions must be consistent with the entire area of social living.[1]

Walter Hoving, in his book, *The Distribution Revolution*,[2] defines America's goal in this way: "The true goal of the American way of life is the creating of a self-reliant, individually responsible, self-disciplined, well-educated and spiritually oriented people."

The goals for secondary education, proclaimed in the Seven Cardinal Principles of Education and redefined in several more recent documents of the American Association of Public School Principals, indicate that education accepts its responsibility in helping individuals to reach the goals of American democracy.

Vocational education has been recognized as an important segment of secondary education and has its distinct role to play in furthering the aims of secondary schools.

This article describes an effort to determine the role of distributive education as a part of these larger philosophies. It is important to note that the question was approached from the standpoint of—what role *should* distributive education play in educating individuals for the good life in an ideal American democracy? Not, what role *does* it play?

The construction of a philosophy of distributive education along the lines indicated above was the first problem to be solved in a research study undertaken in 1965 to determine (1) the competencies a DE teacher coordinator needs to effectively conduct a distributive education program in a secondary school and (2) the experiences that should

[1]Graff, Orin B. and Calvin M. Street. *Improving Competence in Educational Administration*. New York: Harper and Brothers, 1956.

[2]Hoving, Walter. *The Distribution Revolution*. New York: Ives Washburn, Inc., 1960.

be included in a teacher education program to develop these competencies.[3]

Since the distributive education program in 1965 was expanding rapidly and experiencing many changes, the consideration of a philosophy of distributive education as the foundation for the research study was timely. Expansion of the program was due to several factors.

First, the scope of the program had been broadened to encompass the total field of distribution, including retailing, wholesaling, services, and the distributive phases of manufacturing.

Second, the levels of training had been extended to include programs for employees and supervisory, mid-management and management personnel.

Third, the provision for pre-employment training had been established.

Fourth, distributive education had been recognized as a program in which a variety of courses are offered to meet the needs of each level of instruction.

Thus it can be seen that the expansion of the distributive education program was not just a matter of growth in numbers; it involved new concepts and new understandings. Hence it seemed appropriate, in order to arrive at principles to guide the program, to examine basic beliefs concerning all phases of distributive education in light of current happenings in all areas of vocational education.

_____

[3]Entitled "A Competency Pattern Approach to Curriculum Construction in Distributive Teacher Education," the study was funded under Section 4(c) of the Vocational Education Act of 1963. The first phase of the research (reported here) was completed in December 1967.

Design of the Study

The research staff constructed statements concerning basic beliefs in distributive education from the literature and research in distributive and vocational education, from speeches at national clinics and professional meetings, from conferences with selected leaders including DE specialists in the U. S. Office of Education, and from the personal experience of the investigator.

These statements were revised on the basis of suggestions from a committee of consultants composed of acknowledged experts in distributive education, school administration, vocational education, and distribution. Each of the 96 statements of basic beliefs was printed on a card. The 96 cards made up a card-sort which was submitted to the entire population of state supervisory and teacher education personnel.

The thoughtful comments written on the backs of the cards together with a rating to indicate the degree of agreement with each statement made it possible to construct a philosophy of distributive education which reflects the considered opinions of the leadership in the field.

An examination of the _definitions_ and _aims and objectives_ will illustrate the importance of having a philosophical foundation on which to build a program. These definitions and aims and objectives, as agreed upon by the vast majority of DE state supervisory and teacher education personnel, are as follows:

Distributive education: A vocational instructional program designed to meet the needs of persons who have entered or are preparing to enter a distributive occupation or an occupation requiring competency in one or more of the marketing functions. As a vocational program, it offers instruction in marketing, merchandising, related management and personal development.

Distributive occupations: Occupations followed by persons engaged primarily in the marketing or merchandising of goods and services, at both management and nonmanagement levels.

Teacher-coordinator: A member of the local school staff who teaches distributive and related subject matter to students preparing for employment and coordinates classroom instruction with on-the-job training or with occupationally oriented learning activities of students. Is responsible for the distributive education program in the school. Responsibilities for adult distributive education may vary.

Cooperative plan: An organizational pattern of instruction which involves regularly scheduled part-time employment and which gives students an opportunity to apply classroom learnings in practice. Enables students to develop occupational competencies through training on jobs related to their occupational interests.

Project plan: An organizational pattern of instruction which involves a series of selected learning activities or projects related to the field of marketing, merchandising and management and to the student's occupational interests.

Preparatory instruction: Instruction which prepares youth or adults for entry and advancement in a distributive occupation or in an occupation requiring distributive competencies. May be under the project plan or part of the cooperative plan.

Supplementary instruction: Instruction for distributive workers wishing to refresh, update, or upgrade competencies needed in their distributive employment. Usually provided on a part-time basis.

Coordination: The process of organizing, developing, and maintaining effective relationships among all groups involved in the distributive education program to the end that the student receives the best possible preparation for a career in distribution.

Cooperative method: A means by which an organized sequence of on-the-job learning experiences enabling each student to develop competencies related to his occupational interest is correlated with classroom instruction.

Participating experiences: Learning experiences which focus on activities of distributive occupations and decision-making situations in distribution.

Project method: A means by which classroom instruction is correlated with a series of group and/or individually designed learning activities and projects related to a student's occupational interest.

Project: A combination of organized classroom and community learning activities related to an individual's occupational interests. Length of completion time depends upon the ability of the individual learner.

Occupational objective: A current career goal, selected by the student, the preparation for which is the purpose for his vocational instruction in distribution and marketing.

Distributive Education Clubs of America: Youth organization providing a program of activities which complements and enriches distributive curriculums.

Advisory committee: Group of persons representative of both the school and the business community which gives recommendations that may be used for the development and improvement of the distributive education program. School representatives are ex-officio members.

Training sponsor: Person in a distributive organization designated to be responsible for training and supervising the DE student on his job. Works directly with the DE coordinator.

Training station: Place of employment where the DE student receives on-the-job training and supervision by his employer and/or training sponsor.

Aims and Objectives

Preparation for gainful employment and for advancement in a distributive occupation is the primary goal of the distributive education program. The distributive education progam should:

• Engender an understanding and appreciation of the American private enterprise system as a cornerstone of American democracy.

• Foster an awareness of the civic, social, and moral responsibilities of business and society.

• Encourage and promote the use of ethical standards in business and industry.

• Stimulate the DE student's interest in his chosen occupational field by giving him an understanding of the opportunities it offers him to be a contributing member of society.

• Prepare distributive personnel to analyze consumer demand and to satisfy the needs and wants of consumers intelligently, efficiently, and pleasantly.

• Provide training that results in increased efficiency in distribution and marketing.

• Be sensitive to changes in distributive and marketing practices and procedures as they are affected by societal, economic, technical, and educational developments, and adapt to such changes.

• Advance the objectives of the total educational program.

• Strive to develop among employers, employees, and consumers a wider appreciation of the value of specifically trained personnel in distribution.

Implications

Definitions and aims and objectives represent 29 of the 96 basic beliefs concerning distributive education. They, like the beliefs concerning guidance, curriculum, coordination, administration, and teacher education, give direction and purpose to every phase of the distributive education program.

The fact that a large majority of the leadership in distributive education has agreed upon these beliefs indicates that the philosophy of distributive education as expressed in these findings can serve not only as the theoretical structure of the competency study but also as a foundation for what is hoped will be a chain of research to follow.

It may be of value also to researchers in other vocational services for purposes of comparison with philosophies in their own fields—from the standpoint of both the content and the method used in the construction of basic beliefs.

Distributive teacher educators can use the findings as a major source of material for the course in organization and administration of distributive education. DE administrators—national, state and local—should find the philosophical statements helpful in interpreting the program to the public.

Basic beliefs regarding distributive education should become an important segment in any consideration of a philosophy of vocational education.

The objectives as identified and tested in this study, should serve as a guide for all phases of the distributive education program. It should be possible to derive specific teaching objectives from the broad program objectives.

Curriculum workers at every level of the distributive education program can use the findings regarding the basic beliefs of distributive education as a step toward a "curriculum theory model."[4]

[4]Elliott, Davis L. and Arthur W. Foshay. "Chart or Charter: Recent Developments in Educational Discourse," *Review of Educational Research*, citing F. X. C. Northrup, *The Logic of the Sciences and the Humanities* (New York: Meridian Books, 1959).

Changing the Context in which Occupational Education Takes Place

A report by the
Task Force on Vocational-
Technical Education
of the
Education Commission of the
States, with proposals
for consideration by
each of the fifty states*

PART I. WE BELIEVE

1. Public education exists for all the people. Public schools have become a vital link to progress and indeed the very structure of our democratic society.
2. The achievements of America's public schools over the past hundred years have developed potentials for creativity in our society that have brought us to the threshold of a new era in which the possibilities for greatness will be limitless.
3. In this last half of the 20th Century,

* The chairman of the Ad Hoc Committee was Dr. Leon P. Minear, state superintendent of public instruction, Oregon. The chairman of the Steering Committee of the Education Commission of the States is Governor Calvin L. Rampton, Utah, who prepared the foreword for the report.

educated people, and the technology they have fostered, have given this nation a margin of choice which must be used wisely if a society of free men is to endure.
4. The schools are responsible for educating and preparing individuals for full participation in the economic life of American society; thus, the schools have a major responsibility in the field of manpower development.

PART II. WE OBSERVE

1. "Education for *all*" has become a reality; but the formal classroom setting which does not motivate nor serve all the people is still the primary environment for public education. The community, with all its resources, must also be involved as

113

a context in which learning takes place.

2. Generally, education for work life is not treated equally nor simultaneously with education in the intellectual, cultural, social, and political areas of human endeavor.

3. A plethora of educational programs, often poorly related to each other or to "real life," points up the need for strong state leadership in master planning and coordination. The resources unique to each state must be mobilized to provide each individual sufficient numbers and kinds of learning experiences to prepare him to meet society's ever-changing demands.

PART III. WE PROPOSE

1. That a *Human Resources Council* be established in each state.
   - The membership would consist of heads of those departments of state government that each state deemed appropriate, plus key lay citizens. The Chief State School Officer may serve as Executive Secretary.
   - The Council's responsibility would be to develop long-range goals (this might be referred to as a "Bill of Educational Rights and Public Responsibilities") with a view toward adding the community context for education to the present "school" context and relating the two.

   The following principles may guide the Council as it leads in setting the States' educational goals:

   A. *Priority.* Education should be given first priority in the allocation of human and material resources.

   B. *Community Involvement.* Education should be extended outward from the school to the entire community. Citizens can be involved as advisors on policy and programs, as tutors in and out of "school," as resource persons, and as students themselves.

   C. *Extension of School Day and School Year.* Schools, as resource centers for learning for students of all ages, should operate from 8 A.M. to midnight every week of the year.

   D. *Flexible Termination, Reentry, and Advancement.* The formal school-leaving age should be made flexible so that the individual, as he reaches the maturity to either go on to college or a job, may do so with the assurance that pursuit of a liberal education can continue along with career development, throughout life. Both dropouts and graduates whose skills become obsolete could be welcomed back into this kind of system to take up where they once left off, without fear of new failure.

   E. *Individualization of Instruction.* No limitations or inhibitions should be placed summarily on learning because of age, ability or other factors— rather, learning experiences should be planned to meet the needs of the individual.

   F. *Follow-up and Feedback.* Effectiveness of educational programs should be continuously evaluated through a follow-up of all students for an indefinite period and securing feedback on how well the programs are serving their consumers. Such information can be used for program redevelopment and improvement as well as for continual escalation of individual skills.

   - The Council would establish and coordinate the work of state-level commissions which would concentrate upon bringing contextual reform to education in each of the following areas: occupational, social, cultural, political, and intellectual—beginning with occupational.

2. That an *Occupational Education*

Commission be established in each state, with counterparts in Local Community Advisory Councils.[1]

- The Commission would be a top-level group, broadly representative, including members from labor and management in the private sector, as well as from public service. The State Vocational Education Director may serve as Executive Secretary. The Commission would have a full-time professional and clerical staff.

- The Commission's responsibility would be to provide leadership and stimulate development of vocational-technical education programs designed to achieve the goals defined in cooperation with the Human Resources Council, with attention to such factors as:

  - Existing vocational - technical programs in the state upon which improved programs can be built.

  - Size and ecological characteristics of the communities in the state—metropolitan, urban-rural and rural.

  - Identification of individual dropouts and potential dropouts as well as unemployed and underemployed adults. With this group specific training and job entry is of key importance. *This should be the target population* for initial efforts in contextual reform; then the identified "passive" youngsters, and ultimately *all* the youngsters and adults who can benefit.

- Through its counterparts, the Local Community Advisory Councils on Vocational-Technical Education, the Commission would cooperate with local and intermediate school districts and lay citizens to:

  - Survey human resources—state, institutional, group, and individual.

  - Identify, establish, and staff "learning stations"—in order to induct youth and adults into programs including, but not limited to, "school."

  - Develop exploratory and tryout experiences, extend the school day and year, provide for flexible termination and reentry, identify and prepare lay instructors, and develop new curricula.

  - Provide, in cooperation with business, industry, and other agencies, for follow-up and placement of students.

3. That a *Manpower Coordinating Committee* be established in each state.
   - The composition of the Committee should provide for high-level representation of labor and management, and of the appropriate state agencies.
   - The Committee's responsibility would be to effect maximum system-cost effectiveness in the utilization of the various occupational and job training programs.
   - The Committee's primary function should be coordinative rather than administrative, with the actual implementation of the education and training programs being the responsibility of the appropriate agency.
   - A state may elect to have this Committee operate as a subcommittee of the Occupational Education Commission, or separately, with close working relationships with the Commission.

4. That each state consider the establishment of a *Task Force for Occupational Education and Economic Development.*

---

[1] Each state now has a Vocational Education Advisory Council established under Public Law 88-210. The Occupational Education Commission could be the same body, or a reconstituted body, and be asked to assume the responsibilities set forth in this section of the report.

- This Task Force would draw specialists from appropriate existing state agencies (including the Department or Division of Economic Development), labor, management, and the new groups proposed above.

- The responsibility of the Task Force would be to help build up the state's industrial output through new or expanded industries. This would be done by means of providing information to assist industries in considering the state as a site, providing a pool of trained workers, and/or making available undeveloped (or underdeveloped) workers who can be trained for jobs provided by new industries.

- A state may want to consider this kind of special occupational education service if it seems likely that through its use the income of the state could be substantially increased. The Task Force could operate as a subcommittee of the Occupational Education Commission, or separately.

5. That *Regional Learning Centers* be established in each state in Intermediate Education District or County School Offices or other regional educational organizations in the state.

- The Centers would be staffed with student-personnel specialists who would work with sociologists, psychologists, economists, and cultural and political leaders to synthesize educational planning for the region. The Local Community Advisory Councils described in Proposal No. 2 above would work closely with the Centers.

- The responsibility of the Centers would be to provide leadership in development of broad, interdisciplinary curricula that are responsive to the needs of society and the individual and geared to the resources of the region.

- The results of this planning would be used by counselors in diagnosis and prognosis for individual learners, and by master teachers in planning complementary educational experiences in specific fields.

Relationship of Industrial Arts to Occupational Orientation

Donald Maley

Occupational orientation is one of a series of titles attached to a movement that is reaching into nearly all levels of public education as well as into a broad range of school subjects. Other titles in this movement include career education, career development, and occupational education. Even at the national level, there is not a clear and precise definition associated with the concept around which all of these are generated. I will use the terms occupational orientation and occupational education interchangeably throughout this discussion.

The concept of occupational orientation is one of the principle issues in education at this time. Industrial arts must concern itself with this matter, and I have been an out-spoken critic of those who have refused to accept it as a valid function of this area. Occupational education has become a high-priority national issue, a major concern among our top educational planners.

Industrial arts must move more positively in the direction of those national concerns where it can play a significant role, and this is one such concern that has great potential for putting industrial arts out in front. More and more, education will be compelled to focus on societal issues and problems. Industrial arts or any school subject must have a quality of flexibility and adeptness that will enable it to function as a dynamic harmonic with the societal rhythms of change, emphasis, and human need. This is a real and genuine challenge to industrial arts.

Our particular concern is the relationship of occupational orientation to industrial arts. The fluid nature of interpretations associated with the terms may cause serious problems in themselves, but it is worth more and deeper dialogue if education is to seek newer levels of meaning and relevance.

As a point of clarification, the following definition of industrial arts describes the subject area in which the discussion will be based.

Industrial arts as a curriculum area is defined as those phases of general education which deal with *technology*—its evolution, utilization, and significance—with *industry*—its organization, materials, occupations, processes and products—and with the problems and benefits resulting from the technological and industrial nature of society.

Even though the word occupation appears only once in the definition, there is a great deal of relevancy in all facets of the definition as regards occupational education.

A second point of initial clarification deals with one's concept of education and the role of occupational orientation.

One must first get at the goal of occupational orientation. *Why*, as educators, are we interested in this area of national concern? Is it because there is a possibility of a federal grant lurking in the bushes? Is it because we have need for plumbers, carpenters, programmers, welders, shoe salesmen, or service station attendants? Or is it because we have a fundamental and honest desire to fulfill the commitment of education in this democracy?

The goal of education in America is tied to individuals and the enabling of each individual to become what it is possible for him to become as a valued and contributing member of society.

The goal of occupational education must have some relevance to enabling the individual to eventually arrive at that decision which would provide for the greatest degree of compatibility between himself as a human being and the position he chooses to enter as a respectable, productive citizen.

This can be accomplished only if we are willing to start with the assumption that a basic understanding of self is primary. This of course assumes that the individual is to make the decision and that it will be based upon realistic, attainable goals with as broad an understanding of the alternatives as is possible.

Occupational education is not a new topic in discussions related to the content of industrial arts. However, there has not been a uniformity of agreement on the nature and position of such an objective or field of concentration.

The topic has some obvious polar positions that one can easily identify with the industrial arts profession. Although I have tended to develop what some would call a polar position, it is a positive attitude towards the relationship between occupational education and industrial arts.

There is a strong relationship, and the implications for occupational education are important and valid for industrial arts in an era so profoundly affected by industry and technology.

I will attempt to get to this position by the identification of some specific areas of relationship and implication and to identify problems associated with involvement in occupational education in an age when the dynamics of change are literally incomprehensible.

One polar position that has some traditional as well as geographic sources would place industrial arts almost completely in the occupational or specific pre-vocational polar position. The major function of industrial arts would be a narrow pre-vocational emphasis through the development of a select series of manipulative skills and a defined series of informational items aimed at a select series of occupations (*See* Figure 1).

A great deal of occupational education has been external in context. It has tended to stress that which is supposed to be "out there," some remote, vague, inaccessible, and in many instances unattainable goal.

In its attempt to get to the point of being practical and specific, occupational orientation frequently has lost its sense of reality in the fragmented minutia of bits of information, selected manipulative skills and processes.

This posture is illustrated on the right side of Figure 1. However, the left side of that illustration deserves concerted study.

We in education (not just industrial arts) should give serious consideration to the development in each individual of some fundamental understandings about his potential, his capabilities, his emotional and psychological qualities. This is the only starting point. Starting with the individual as the center of

119

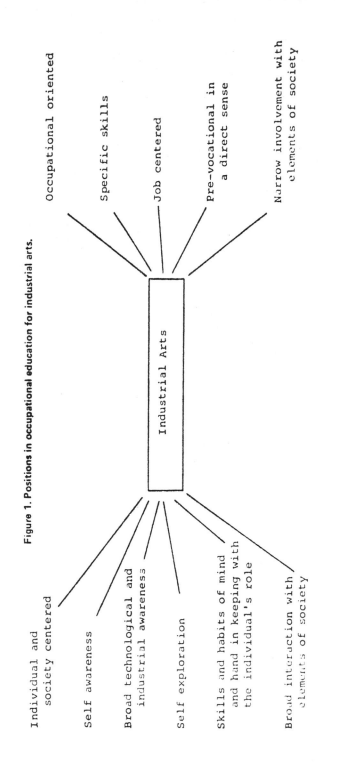

Figure 1. Positions in occupational education for industrial arts.

Occupational oriented

Specific skills

Job centered

Pre-vocational in a direct sense

Narrow involvement with elements of society

Industrial Arts

Individual and society centered

Self awareness

Broad technological and industrial awareness

Self exploration

Skills and habits of mind and hand in keeping with the individual's role

Broad interaction with elements of society

focus should constitute the initial concern.

This can happen only if we sincerely believe in it and are willing to put out time, talents, and facilities to its accomplishment. Industrial arts cannot accomplish all that needs to be done in this regard. However, no other area has an environmental and pedagogical-philosophical arena comparable to that of the industrial arts laboratory in which to work with people as individuals. The profession should move more broadly out into the arena of contemporary society for the background, information, and trends against which a course of action may be plotted.

Occupational education in the contemporary setting must concern itself with the following elements.
1. The changing occupational structure
2. The increasing mobility of people
3. The need for adaptability in people
4. The issue of occupational obsolescence
5. The phenomena of technological impact
6. The changing social patterns
7. The effects of technological developments
8. The long-range outlook
9. The population growth
10. The changing educational patterns

The discussion of occupational education and its relationship to industrial arts is an involvement in diversity with countless and varied occupations, a concern for a role for industrial arts, and a perspective on education in the contemporary society and the years ahead.

A recent edition of the *Dictionary of Occupational Titles* lists a total of 21,741 occupations. This figure contains 6,432 jobs new to the dictionary. Of interest and pertinence also is the fact that there are 8,000 fewer titles in the new volume (Ref. 2, p. 9). This is due to jobs becoming obsolete and the combining of several jobs into a single title.

The industrial arts student body consists of nearly every male at the junior high school level and a somewhat smaller proportion in the senior high school. Industrial arts is not dealing with just the future manufacturing personnel in the categories of laborers, craftsmen, foremen, or operatives. It is dealing with all segments of the population, which includes the increasing numbers who will go into the human services, sales, managerial, clerical, technical, and the professional areas.

A third bit of information that needs to receive our attention is the trend of the occupational structure in the United

States. Figure 2 depicts the change in percentage of the total labor market over a twenty-four year period for farm workers, service workers, white collar workers, and blue collar workers.

Figure 2. Change in distribution of employment by major occupation groups, 1947-71.

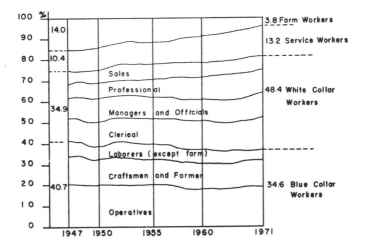

Figure 3 represents the structure of the work force as viewed by Dr. Norman Harris of the University of Michigan. This figure is radically different than the pyramid configuration that was so characteristic of the structure some few years ago.

A fourth very important factor involves the rate and nature of change due to technological, economic, sociological, and political developments. The increased productivity per man, the knowledge and population explosions, the rise of social issues, and the increasing emphasis on education also are essential factors in a consideration of occupational education, for it (occupational education) does not exist in a vacuum, nor should it lie static while society continues to move.

These broad areas of concern give rise to several basic questions that one might raise in the process of developing ideas for implementing meaningful and relevant occupational education through the industrial arts programs.

122

Figure 3. Work force, 1970; projected by Dr. Norman C. Harris, University of Michigan.

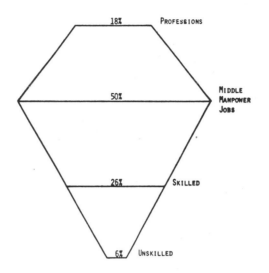

The Problem of Number and Diversity of Occupations in Relation to the Capability for Occupational Education in Industrial Arts

There are from 21 to 22 thousand different occupations in the United States. If industrial arts is to be serious about any "specific" occupational education, what infinitesimally small part of these thousands of occupations can it really deal with in the time allotted?

The Problem of the Proportion of the Population Served and The Proportion of the Population Needed to Produce the Goods

We are told that by the year 2000 it will require only 2 to 3% of the work force to produce the goods that will be needed. If this becomes a reality, and the example set by agriculture leads us to believe it will, what will industrial arts' function be in a curriculum area that serves 40 to 47% of the total junior high school population (males) and has aspirations to serving nearly all of that population (both boys and girls)?

The relationship of the proportion of the population served by industrial arts to the proportion of the population that will be needed to produce the goods must be considered.

The Problem of Occupational Change Due to Advances in Technology and Fundamental Changes in the Society

We are told that the rapidity of change experienced in the past 25 years is just a prelude to that which lies ahead. The acceleration of change in science, industry, and technology has opened many new areas of occupational endeavor. This movement also has changed rather substantially thousands of occupations and greatly reduced the need for numerous others (*See* Figure 4).

Figure 4.

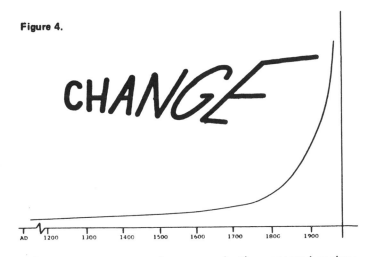

As man moves away from a production-centered society into a service mode and in the direction of solving man's pressing problems, new and vastly different issues will face the educator dealing with occupational education. This is especially true in a general education subject that has industry and technology for its base of content.

Some years ago this nation moved out of an agricultural economy into an industrial society. We have now moved into a post-industrial or super-industrial society, and the weight of the economy has shifted from production to services.

Substantial increases in employment have been experienced in the social services, health services, recreation, science, engineering, administration, accounting, and controlling fields.

The dimension and nature of industrial arts involvement in occupational education is the issue that needs to be explored and the systems of involvement developed.

124

The Vocational Act of 1963 has had a significant role in a changing pattern of education and occupational preparation. We have witnessed the development of extensive and elaborate vocational facilities in area and comprehensive high schools, as well as at the post-high school level. This has given the high school industrial arts program breathing space and the opportunity to really stretch its image in the area of general education aimed at interpreting the industrial and technological nature of the society, as well as contributing to the growth and development of the individuals it serves.

There are three broad areas in which industrial arts can make a significant contribution in the area of occupational orientation.

1. *The first and most important area of contribution is in the realm of the "self."*

Occupational orientation, occupational education, career education, career development, or whatever title you may select can only start at one point, and that is with the individual. Effective career planning must start with an understanding of the "self."

This point, of course, is based on the obvious assumption that the individual makes his own decision regarding his future life's work. This might be an impossible dream for some, but it should be standard operating practice for most people.

Occupational education must start with the individual getting the fullest opportunity to understand himself in terms of his aptitudes, capabilities, interests, mental and physical characteristics, as well as the numerous other personal factors that relate to individual success, contribution, and happiness.

The school has a particularly unique role to play in this process by providing the environment and a program that makes these realizations possible. The industrial arts area, with its endless range of potentially meaningful human involvement, is a natural setting for making a rich contribution to occupational education in the area of self-exploration.

Some years ago at the Los Angeles Convention of the American Industrial Arts Association, Dr. Walter Waetjen presented an address titled "The Exploratory Function of Industrial Arts Education." A portion of this address with particular relevance to self-exploration was as follows:

> That is, exploration, rather than being a series of exposures to formal or "canned" experience is, instead, a technique to be learned as one approaches a new situation . . .

The second alternative has been suggested by educators who have stated in a variety of ways that the over-arching objective of education is to produce people who can live with satisfaction to themselves and of benefit to their society. This objective has an exact parallel in the psychological definition of a well-adjusted person who, according to some psychologists, is one who fulfills his needs in ways which are both self-satisfying and acceptable to society. In each of these definitions there is a word germane to the present discourse. That word is *self*.

Samual Osipow, in a discussion of Donald Super's theories of career development, considers the concept of self-knowledge in relation to deciding on an occupational goal at the ninth-grade level.

... This self-knowledge could be developed without specifically deciding on an occupational goal, which would be premature in the ninth grade. In fact, rather than restrict occupational possibilities at that age, the school should exert its efforts to broaden the student's occupational perspectives and to teach him to use available resources for exploration effectively (Ref. 3, p. 132).

Corollary to the "self-knowledge" precept is the juxtaposition of the development of the individual with respect to the timing of his industrial arts experiences.

In an attempt to establish a "time-line" or chronological justification for the role of industrial arts at the junior high school level, I have extracted a number of statements from an article titled: "The Critical Ninth Grade: Vocational Choice or Vocational Exploration," by Donald Super (Ref. 4, pp. 108, 109).

If people are to make choices, they must have attitudes, an orientation toward life in general, toward careers in particular, and toward their present life stage especially, which facilitate the consideration of alternatives and the making of the required decisions ... (pg. 108).

As to the matter of readiness to make vocational choices, he comments that

Ninth graders are clearly in an exploratory stage, not in a decision-making stage, of vocational development ... (pg. 108).

Early in his article, Super raised the question of "early identification for what?", and this is his reply.

... not early identification for vocational choice or selection, but early identification for vocational exploration ... the identification of vocational potential in ninth graders should be designed to help with the making of decisions for vocational exploration rather than decisions of vocational preparation (pg. 109).

The obvious points made by Dr. Super were in the realm of attitudes, orientation, and exploration. These are important and viable components or goals of a good industrial arts program.

2. Since the "self" as an organism does not live in a vacuum, it is imperative that the individual develop societal awareness as extensively as possible. This is the second leg in the triangle associated with the contribution of industrial arts to the process of occupational orientation.

A prime requisite for effective participation in any society is to have a basic understanding of as many as possible of the elements that impinge upon the "decision" area(s).

The door is wide open for both the junior and senior high school programs to provide an instructional program relevant to the much-needed involvement with and interpretation of industry and technology.

The relationship of this goal of industrial and technological awareness with occupational education is direct and positive. An industrial arts program that provides a comprehensive involvement in a broad study of major industries is a vehicle for increasing the awareness of opportunities, conditions, contributions, and requirements associated with the world of work.

This same awareness can be developed in the various technologies associated with communications, power generation, construction, production, and the utilization of the natural resources.

The key to this contributory element of "developing an awareness" is to make every effort to reach out in program and student involvement so that the goal of occupational education has the width and breadth required to be of any assistance to the individual where freedom of choice and mobility are part of the system.

No other activity in the school experience has the potential for opening vistas in a technological society and the world of industry comparable to that of industrial arts. It can be a realistic and concrete experience as well as extensive "role involvement" in producing, planning, organizing, researching, and evaluating, in addition to the social aspects of industry, in a manner that has little resemblance to the canned lectures, films, or essays on occupations so commonly employed in the area of occupational education.

3. The third area is "functional skills," the very important arena wherein the "power" and impact of the individual on his environment is developed. Specifically, it includes the follow-

ing ideas with respect to the individual:

- the development of the manual and manipulative skills,
- the development of skills in problem solving and resourcefulness,
- the development of communication skills,
- the development of skills in social interaction, leadership, followership, cooperation, and involved participation.

The relationship of industrial arts to occupational education can be visualized in the form of an equilateral triangle, with each leg providing an important interface with the other two.

1. The first side is the development of as full an *understanding of the self* as is possible.
2. The second side is devoted to a broadening *awareness of the world around the individual*.
3. The third side is the development of *fundamental skills* which contribute to the realization of each individual's potential as well as his aspirations.

Each of these deals with the general educational development of people with no specific identification of fixed manipulative skills, jobs, or occupations. They are in essence broad areas of competence or understanding vital to effective occupational orientation. Each of these contributes to the realization of individuals, regardless of the nature and rate of change with which they are confronted. Each is basic and fundamental to the ultimate goal of occupational education.

The following quotation by Arthur W. Combs is a statement of a goal of education that has direct relationship to the point of this presentation:

"The goal of education must be self-actualization, the production of persons willing and able to interact with the world in intelligent ways. To achieve that end, educators must concern themselves with both halves of the equation: the person and the world, the learner and the subject . . ." (Ref. 1, p. vi).

Industrial arts can and must demonstrate its capability in the national concern for occupational orientation. The opportunity and the capability are there and all that is necessary is the resolve to do it.

Think in broad terms that will meet the challenge of society characterized by unprecedented change and growth. The narrower you get in your perspective, the more you are inclined to play games with the lives of young people caught up in a captive system.

128

Bibliography

1. Combs, Arthur W. "Foreword," *Humanizing Education: The Person in the Process.* Washington, D.C.: Association for Supervision and Curriculum Development, N.E.A., 1967.
2. Eckerson, A. B. "What's New in the D O T?" *Employment Service Review.* Vol. 3, No. 3, p. 9; March, 1966.
3. Osipow, Samual, *Theories of Career Development.* New York: Appleton-Century-Crofts, 1968.
4. Super, Donald E., "The Critical Ninth Grade: Vocational Choice or Vocational Exploration", *Personnel and Guidance Journal.* 39:106-109, October, 1960.

NEW DESIGNS
IN VOCATIONAL
& PRACTICAL
ARTS
EDUCATION

J. Robert Warmbrod

THE INFLUENCE of the Vocational Education Act of 1963 on public school education in the Central states is clearly evident. Although some of the new designs in vocational and technical education are not a direct outgrowth of the national legislation, most of the major changes currently taking place are influenced, in no small part, by the act that proclaims it to be national policy "that persons of all ages in all communities . . . will have ready access to vocational training or retraining which is of high quality."

Area Schools. One of the most significant new designs is the establishment of area schools—junior colleges, vocational-technical schools, and technical institutes—in a region of the country where public education of less than baccalaureate level has been traditionally oriented to and controlled by local communities.

Illinois is establishing a statewide system of comprehensive junior colleges authorized by legislation which specifies that at least 15 percent of all courses must be in "occupational, semi-technical, or technical fields leading directly to employment." During 1966-67, seven of some 40 area vocational high schools planned for the state were established.

Indiana established the Indiana Vocational Technical College in 1963 for the purpose of developing post-high school vocational and technical education in the state. A tentative regional organization of technical institutes has been developed. Area vocational schools are also being established to serve high school pupils and adults.

Iowa presently has in operation 11 of an anticipated 16 comprehensive community colleges that offer liberal arts courses in addition to a vocational and technical program.

Kansas has 14 area vocational-technical schools resulting from legislation in 1963 which had as its purpose the establishment of a system of vocational education to serve the entire state.

Kentucky currently has 14 area vocational-technical schools in operation. It is anticipated that in five years, area vocational school facilities will be constructed within commuting distance of most high schools.

Michigan provided post-high school programs in vocational and technical education in 18 community colleges and five four-year colleges during 1965-66. Studies are under way in 63 of the 83 counties of the state to develop area programs on the high school level.

Minnesota currently operates 24 area schools with programs primarily for post-high school students. Plans for area vocational-technical schools, first established in Minnesota in 1945, indicate that by 1970, 90 percent of the population will be within 35 miles of an area school.

Missouri has approved the establishment of 30 area vocational schools to serve high school, post-high school, and adult students.

Nebraska has two state-operated vocational-technical schools in addition to the School of Technical Agriculture, a two-year post-secondary school established in 1965 to serve the entire state. Locally operated area schools that serve several counties are being established under the provisions of legislation enacted in 1965.

North Dakota has one area school, located in the southeastern part of the state, which serves the entire state.

Ohio has established 24 joint vocational schools under the provisions of legislation that permits the establishment of joint vocational school districts in small cities and rural areas.

South Dakota, through legislation enacted in 1965, has designated six areas for the establishment of area vocational-technical schools.

Wisconsin's system of independent vocational school districts, established in 1911, includes 15 technical institutes, 26 vocational schools, and 22 vocational evening schools operated by autonomous local boards of vocational and technical education. The 1965 General Assembly directed that all areas of the state be included in independent vocational school districts by 1970.

Uses of New Funds. The development of area programs of vocational and technical education has led to larger allocations of funds, both federal and state, for constructing and equipping area schools. Minnesota allocates from 30 to 50 percent of the additional funds received under the provisions of the Vocational Education Act of 1963 for such construction.

During 1965-66, Ohio allocated over $6 million for construction and equipment in 14 area vocational school districts. During the same year, Michigan made grants totaling $5 million for area construction projects, with approximately two-thirds going to community colleges.

Additional funds are used also to develop new programs in health occupations, business and office education, vocational guidance, and technical education. The development of programs for persons with special needs is receiving major emphasis.

State Appropriations. State appropriations for vocational and technical education are increasing more rapidly than allotments of federal funds. State appropriations in Minnesota increased from $4,350,000 for fiscal year 1965 to an estimated $8,300,000 for fiscal year 1967. The Missouri General Assembly in its last session increased state funds for vocational education by 20 percent. In Kentucky state appropriations for fiscal 1967 indicate a 38-percent increase over the preceding year.

State appropriations earmarked

specifically for the construction of area vocational-technical schools are making their appearance. Kentucky has passed a $3,400,000 bond issue for construction of area vocational-technical schools. Iowa legislation in 1965 included an appropriation of $6 million for the construction of area vocational-technical schools and community colleges.

Organizational Changes. Several state departments of education have changed their organizational structures to give a more prominent role to vocational and technical education. The establishment of a state board of vocational and technical education by Indiana's General Assembly in 1965 led to the creation of a vocational-technical division. Separate divisions of vocational and technical education, directed by an assistant commissioner, have been established also in Missouri and Minnesota.

Illinois, Michigan, Minnesota, and Wisconsin have reorganized their vocational and technical divisions in an effort to find a structure more functional than the former organization by occupational categories.

A concomitant development is the addition of new staff positions in vocational guidance and counseling, programs for persons with special needs, work-study, manpower training, business and office education, and research.

New Programs. New designs in vocational and technical education in the Central states emphasize program developments involving several occupational areas. A notable example is the experimental preparatory program at Paola, Kansas. (See article on page 28 of this issue.)

The development of educational programs involving several occupational areas has been facilitated by establishing program development units at the state level and staffing them with specialists in all areas of vocational education.

Special attention is given to the development of programs to serve pupils in small high schools where the availability of a wide range of vocational offerings has been limited. Illinois has developed "interrelated cooperative education" programs to serve pupils from two or more occupational fields in a common course. Minnesota and Nebraska are developing "diversified occupations" programs to provide instruction in a variety of occupations. A research project is in progress at Michigan State University to develop programs of vocational education appropriate to small schools.

Curriculum development and the preparation of instructional materials are receiving high priority. Ohio has established instructional materials laboratories for trade and industrial education, distributive education, and agricultural education.

A project is underway at the University of Illinois to develop curriculum guides for high school programs which integrate instruction in homemaking and family life with preprofessional and employment education in home economics. A major project at Michigan State University involves the development of instructional materials for all occupational areas.

Pilot, experimental, and demonstration projects are used widely in the Central states for developing, evaluating, and implementing new vocational and technical education programs. Supervised occupational experience in business and industry is recognized as an essential element of the new and emerging programs. Wide-spread use of local, area, and statewide advisory groups is evident.

Student organizations continue to develop as an integral part of programs of vocational and technical education for both high school and post-high school students.

Agricultural Occupations. Major emphasis in agricultural education is placed on the development of programs for off-farm occupations involving knowledge and skill in agricultural subjects. Pilot programs have been conducted to develop programs in horticulture, agricultural mechanics, agricultural supply, and agricultural business. A demonstration center has been established at Reidland High School, Paducah, Ky., for training high school pupils in off-farm agricultural occupations.

Illinois reports that 30 percent of the eleventh- and twelfth-grade pupils studying agriculture in 1966-67 are enrolled in courses oriented toward employment in off-farm business and industries. Agricultural education in horticulture, agricultural mechanics, and programs for persons with special needs is expanding to city school systems. For example, an extensive program in horticulture is in operation in Cleveland.

New programs in agricultural education in area schools have been limited primarily to post-high school programs.

In 1966-67, 10 of the 13 Central states were offering programs in technical education in agriculture in 47 post-high school institutions. Technical programs offered include agricultural mechanics, ornamental horticulture, agricultural business, forestry, food processing, park and recreation management, conservation, and farm and ranch management.

Business and Office. Reimbursed vocational programs in business and office education have been established for the first time in most states during the last two years. Programs at the high school level include general clerical, secretarial and stenographic science, data processing, business machine operation, and bookkeeping.

Every state reports rapid development of technical programs in business and office education in area schools and junior colleges. Michigan and Missouri offer specialized medical, dental, and legal secretarial curriculums in junior colleges. Kansas and Wisconsin provide post-high school programs in court and conference reporting. Ohio emphasizes technical programs in data processing, computer programing, and accounting. Other post-high school programs offered are stenography, executive secretarial science, and middle-level office management.

Distributive Occupations. All states are experiencing substantial growth in high school preparatory programs in distributive education. Michigan State University is conducting a pilot project which compares the results of the regular cooperative program with a preparatory program based on the project method and simulated situations. Post-high school programs concentrate on specialized programs with specific orientation to preparation for middle-management positions.

Health Occupations. Dramatic growth is anticipated in health education; however, most of these programs are emerging in post-high school institutions. Among them are programs for licensed practical nurses, associate degree programs for nurses, and programs for dental hygienists, dental laboratory technicians, psychiatric aides, occupational therapy assistants, nurses' aides, operating room technicians, geriatrics care aides, hospital ward clerks, and residential child care aides.

An area high school in Chicago has cooperative programs for nurses' aides, blood bank assistants, and hospital supply aides.

Home Economics. Emphasis in home economics education is on the development of programs for gainful employment. Every state is developing high school programs for wage earning occupations in food service, child care, clothing construction and alteration. dietary aides, nursing home workers, hotel and motel workers, and homemaker's assistant.

Michigan provides post-high school programs in food technology, institutional management, food cost control, and food purchasing. Iowa has a post-high school program in fashion merchandising; Minnesota offers interior design. Wisconsin is developing post-high school programs for assistants to professional home economists employed in business and industry. Illinois offers child development in junior colleges.

Post-high school programs are provided also for assistant dieticians, food service supervisors, fashion designers, and child care assistants.

Technical Occupations. Technical education, both in the occupational areas described and in engineering and industrial occupations, is in a period of rapid expansion in the Central states. Last January the Ohio Center for Research and Leadership Development held a national conference to identify new and emerging technical occupations and to determine critical areas for technical education research.

New programs in engineering and industrial technology include aeronautical and aviation electronics, architectural technology, numerical control for the metal working industries, chemical technology, city planning, instrumentation, engineering drafting, commercial art and layout technology, tool design technology, and commercial aviation.

Trade and Industrial. The recent growth of trade and industrial education has been greatest in area vocational-technical schools. Enrollment in area schools in Kansas and Kentucky is primarily in industrial education programs. Minnesota is developing new programs in industrial education in area schools for high school pupils. Area schools are used

in Missouri to promote trade and industrial education in communities not previously served.

A new design is the "galaxy approach" for teaching industrial education in the high schools of Detroit. In this approach the instructional program is based on a grouping of knowledge and manipulative skills into four major areas: materials and processes, visual communications, energy and propulsion, and personal services.

Nebraska uses the "cluster concept" for industrial education at the high school level.

Adult Education. Rapid expansion is occurring in vocational and technical programs for persons who have entered the labor market and need training or retraining. Adult education is growing rapidly in area schools.

Illinois, Kansas, Nebraska, and Ohio indicate that adult education in business and office occupations is being expanded. Nebraska offers classes for adults in wage earning occupations in home economics. Apprenticeship classes are being expanded in Wisconsin. Missouri has recently developed adult programs in automotive mechanics and body repair, radio and television repair, and air conditioning and refrigeration. Kansas is adding programs for young farmers in farm business analysis.

Programs for licensed practical nurses are conducted in several states.

Special-Needs Programs. The end is clearly in sight for the time when the needs of the disadvantaged student are accommodated solely by adjustments in regular programs of vocational instruction. Most of the states have added supervisors or consultants for program development in this area.

Michigan conducts practical training programs designed to hold potential dropouts in high school. Minnesota conducts programs for persons with special needs in distributive occupations, office occupations, home economics, and technical education. Welfare recipients in Missouri are getting courses—preparatory to employment training—in reading, spelling and mathematics. Ohio uses laboratory programs which combine work skills and basic education for serving the disadvantaged. Wisconsin conducts special programs in area schools for migrant workers and functionally illiterate adults. Illinois has prevocational courses in industrial education for underachievers and courses in home economics for pupils who are mentally handicapped. Nebraska has designed courses in agricultural mechanics for special education students.

Many of the special education programs are concentrated in the metropolitan areas; however, a current research project at the University of Illinois is designed to develop vocationally oriented programs for rural youth who are economically and socially handicapped.

Guidance and Counseling. During the past three years almost every state has employed specialists in vocational guidance and counseling for state divisions of vocational and technical education.

Michigan and Missouri have conducted regional conferences on vocational counseling for school administrators and counselors. Nebraska, in cooperation with the State Employment Service and the Department of Labor, recently held conferences on occupational opportunities in agriculture for high school counselors.

During 1965-66, pilot programs in vocational guidance were conducted in 32 high schools and post-high school institutions in Illinois. Vocational guidance counselors are being added to area schools staffs in Kentucky, Minnesota, and Wisconsin.

Teacher Education. Plans for the preparation of teachers for new and emerging programs of vocational and technical education are being developed. Teacher education programs in business and office education have recently been established in Missouri, Nebraska, and Indiana. Kentucky is initiating teacher education programs in health occupations, distributive education, and vocational guidance.

A new pattern of vocational teacher education which utilizes the clinical school concept is being developed at Michigan State University. New programs for preparing teachers of technical education are in operation at Kearney State College, Kansas, and Purdue University.

The University of Minnesota and Purdue University have revised teacher education programs in home economics to provide experiences with pupils who are socially and economically disadvantaged. An experimental program is being conducted at the University of Illinois to prepare industrial education teachers to conduct classes for dropout-prone youth.

Major revisions are being made in teacher education in agriculture and home economics. The University of Missouri established a position in home economics education to develop a teacher education program for teachers who will conduct employment education in home economics. The University of Wisconsin is developing an option for students who want to teach wage earning programs in home economics.

The teacher education curriculum at Michigan State University has been revised to provide specialist teachers in agricultural business, agricultural mechanics, and ornamental horticulture. Ohio State University offers an internship program in agricultural education which includes directed occupational experience in business and industry. A postgraduate teacher internship in agricultural education has been established at the University of Wisconsin.

Courses in the organization and development of post-high school programs in business and distributive education are now offered at Ohio State University and the University of Minnesota. The University of Missouri has a graduate program for persons preparing for administrative positions in technical education in junior colleges. Indiana State University has a new program for directors of vocational education.

Inservice education to upgrade teachers for new and emerging programs is receiving major emphasis. An interdisciplinary training program for teachers of the socio-economically handicapped was conducted at the University of Missouri in 1966. In the same year, a training program involving directed occupational experience was offered at the University of Minnesota for teachers of distribution and marketing.

Numerous summer workshops have been held for teachers involved in off-farm agricultural occupations and several states have conducted summer institutes to prepare home economics teachers to develop programs for wage-earning occupations.

R & D. No aspect of vocational and technical education has been influenced by the 1963 Act to a greater extent than research and development. Funds appropriated under section 4(c) of the Act led to the establishment of the Center for Research and Leadership Development at Ohio State University. In addition, federal funds support research coordinating units in 12 of the 13 Central states.

Federal funds also support extensive research and development programs at Iowa State University and Michigan State University.

Numerous training, research, and experimental projects are also being carried out under federal grants.

A grant from the Ford Foundation established the Center for Studies in Vocational and Technical Education at the University of Wisconsin in 1964.

Program development in the Central states can be attributed to systematic study and research carried on to an unprecedented extent. Recommendations for strengthening vocational and technical education in Missouri are the outgrowth of a statewide study ordered by the Governor.

Statewide manpower studies for use in program planning and development were recently completed in North Dakota, Illinois, and Michigan. Research coordinating units are making progress in stimulating research activity and program innovation. State funds, and funds earmarked for ancillary services under the provisions of section 4(a) of the 1963 Act, are used to support research and development activities.

During fiscal 1967, the Illinois Research Coordinating Unit supported research, experimental, and development projects with combined budgets exceeding $1 million. In several other states, research coordinating units have conducted workshops to increase the competence of local administrators, vocational directors and teachers in planning and conducting pilot and demonstration programs. Research relating to evaluation is underway in a number of states.

The Future. Only a few of the many possible new designs can be cited here. Yet the evidence is convincing; the future is bright.

The older, well-established programs are being strengthened and improved; new programs are being developed "in light of actual or anticipated opportunities for gainful employment."

The development of programs "for persons who have academic, socio-economic, or other handicaps" is beginning to receive the attention warranted.

The findings of research are applied to the problems of vocational and technical education to an extent not evident up to this time.

New patterns of organization and administration will enhance the possibility "that persons of all ages in all communities will have ready access to vocational training or retraining which is of high quality."

Industrial Arts —

An Educational Responsibility

for Interpreting Technology

Bill Wesley Brown

Industrial arts education is part of a system of education that is so large and complex that an apt comparison is difficult to describe. I propose to speak in general terms about our total educational enterprise, and then to concentrate on industrial arts—what it is, what it does, its strengths, its weaknesses—and to describe how it fits into the educational scheme of things. If our discussions today and tomorrow are to be of value, in large measure this value will depend upon our understanding of the job of industrial arts as a part of education. In order to assure this understanding—and being mindful of the variety of knowledge and experience that each of you brings to this forum—I am going to assume that you all are visitors to planet Earth. You have come to examine our way of life, and you will report back to your own people about what we do in education.

Historical

In the early development of mankind, education took place in the family unit. Fathers taught sons; mothers taught daughters. In the grinding manner of primitive peoples, our ancestors had to spend most of their waking hours attempting to provide food, fiber, and shelter in order to keep the family unit functioning. We can only imagine a father spending long hours demonstrating to his sons how to fashion a crude weapon or other device to be used in killing an animal for food; the mother teaching the daughter how to care for the hides of animals so that some protection could be obtained from inclement weather. But whatever they did, they did everything for themselves.

From what we have been able to determine, however, the tendency for man to specialize was soon asserting itself. Silt-covered clay tablets have been found in the ruins of ancient Babylonia which spell out articles of apprenticeship. This form of education has endured to this day. It is obvious, however, that a great deal of specialization on the part of some artisans and tradespeople had already taken place well before a great flood. With the advent of the industrial revolution—whereby animal and human muscle power was replaced by inanimate machine power—and the development of mass production techniques and the factory system established in history, specialization increased at an unimaginable pace.

Now people no longer worked as a family unit to directly provide for food, fiber, and shelter. People no longer had to spend most of their waking hours in a never-ending quest for these essentials. But they did find they had to purchase—with money earned in the factory—goods and services the family had formerly provided. One of these services was and is education.

Education can be of many descriptions: general or special, formal or informal, costly or economical, and it can be good or bad. Man found it convenient to invent schools—buildings where those to be taught could gather at appointed times, where instruction could take place, and from which those who have been taught—variously called students, scholars, pupils, and the like—then depart for their homes. Waiting for the students at the schools are those who will teach. These men and women are especially-prepared individuals who have acquired certain skills and knowledge deemed worthy of passing on to each generation. In some schools, students remain in a single room with a single teacher; in other schools, each teacher remains in a single room, and students go to the teacher. Signals such as bells or buzzers announce when teachers should cease instructing one group of students and begin instructing others.

Certain schools have been established to cater to the special needs of a carefully-selected group of students. Hence, we have elementary schools for students from ages 5 or 6 up to 11 or 12, junior high schools for students from 12 or 13 up to 14 or 15, senior high schools for students from 14 or 15 up to 17 or 18, community colleges from 17 or 18 up to 19 or 20, and colleges and universities from 17 or 18 up to whatever age the student decides to leave formal schooling. An AB degree is generally earned by age 21 or 22. Any graduate study is added onto the years of undergraduate study.

Just as many of you have found it economical and convenient to concentrate the production or processing of one item at one location, educators have found it expedient to concentrate their teaching efforts around one general topic—usually called a subject. When the numbers of students and teachers have reached a certain minimal level, departments of that subject have been created. Individuals with great insight, complete honesty, unquestioned integrity, exhaustive mastery of their subject matter, and possessed of miraculous ability to solve personnel, academic, and other problems are hired to manage these departments and schools.

Kinds of Education

Education has historically been one of two kinds—either general or special. In our society and schools, general education has come to mean those educational experiences which are common to all for a given school, department, or unit. Required courses are obviously general education. We can consider all experiences at the elementary level to be general education. Special education has come to mean educational experiences which are elective on the part of some students. With certain notable exceptions, these elective courses are found at the secondary level and beyond. We can also have the apparent dichotomy of a subject appearing to be both general and special education. Music is an excellent case in point. A class in music appreciation required for all eighth grade students is obviously a course in general education. Students who elect to participate in the concert band, however, are engaged in special education. A student who is participating in a class of required physical education is deriving general education values; another student participating in varsity athletics is benefiting from special education. A student participating in industrial arts is in general education; a student in vocational industrial education is in special education. We have already noted that the elementary school provides experiences which are largely general in nature. When a student progresses to the junior high school, he finds that much of his program of studies is still general in nature, but the opportunity for electing different experiences—especially extra-curricular activities—is now present. We also find that male students are generally required to enroll in industrial arts classes and female students are generally required to enroll in home economics classes, the assumption being that females are not a part of our industrial society and that males are not a part of the home.

In many secondary schools today, three options are available to students as they consider their course of study. These include college preparatory, vocational, and general. Regardless of the program chosen, the state of California—or your home state—will specify experiences or courses which must be met if that school is to be an approved school. Local boards of education may, at their discretion, require additional experiences or courses, but they may not reduce the minimal requirements already established by the state.

Educational Expectations

The question of how best to educate young people has caused some of our greatest philosophers and learned men to spend lifetimes developing theories or models of education and learning which others might follow with satisfaction to all. Each has had its adherents, and each—in the fullness of time— has been blunted and shaped by circumstances, people, events, and either the presence or absence of funds. The hopes and expectations of every generation of Americans have been laid at the steps of our school buildings, and with few exceptions, those dreams have been realized.

For some, education has been preparation for additional study at a college or university—in effect delaying the moment when those individuals become contributing members of our industrial-technological society. For others, education has been preparation for securing a job in the society; and for still others, education has been something to do while waiting for inspiration to strike.

We might as well state it as plainly as possible: We live in an industrial-technological society, and all the wishing of some who yearn for a less demanding, agrarian, simplistic society will not make it change. The people in this society have created the highest standard of living yet achieved by mankind.

I am very aware of the potential for both good and bad which is inherent to an industrial-technological society. It is an indictment against cultured, civilized man as a so-called free agent which allows him to use an instrument designed for positive values as an instrument for negative values. Consider for a moment some of the most significant contributions of mankind devised during this century: mass-produced goods, rapid land transport, jet aircraft, the release and control of nuclear energy, electronic communications, the computer, men on the moon, advances in medicine such as heart transplants and the Salk vaccine against the ravages of polio . . . and we could continue. With few exceptions, man could use any of these for constructive and destructive purposes.

In the process of developing this industrial-technological society, we have put together an industrial machine which, not long ago, finally produced a trillion dollar economy. In the process of buying educational services, we have put together an educational system that is also without peer. We, for example, enroll more college students in one institution of higher learning in New York than are enrolled in the entire country of England.

It seems reasonable to ask: "Where in this advanced system of education do the students learn about this incredibly complex industrial-technological society?" The answer is deceptively simple. Either the students learn about our industrial-technological society in industrial arts classes, or they don't study about it. Some explanation is in order. By way of review, you will recall we said that all education is either general or special. Industrial arts is a study about our industrial-technological society; it is taught in our public schools for purposes of general education values—that is, every student, both male and female, since they are a part of an industrial-technological society, ought to study industrial arts. As I see it, industrial arts ought to be required, rather than elective, since by definition industrial arts is the study of our technological tools, materials, processes, successes, and failures. When any subject—industrial arts included—becomes elective, it automatically becomes special education—or at least largely so. Special education is restrictive education—restrictive in terms of the numbers of students able to profit from the instruction. A very real danger exists today because large numbers of students graduate from our secondary schools who will take their places somewhere in their industrial-technological society, and they will never have studied about the greatest system of productivity yet devised by man.

Those of us who have witnessed the phenomenon of campus unrest and wanton destruction of educational facilities on the part of a few so-called students recognize that those who burn and bomb are those who have had little contact with their industrial-technological society. These mental midgets rant and rage against alleged misdeeds and imagined injustices of a "non-humanistic, materialistic system." And their posturing becomes absurd. Is it possible that these misunderstandings, or lack of understanding, could have been avoided if these people had been exposed to a well-taught, thoughtfully-presented industrial arts program? In these classes, they could have learned where and how they could fit into the society in a positive manner. It is entirely possible that some would still be disenchanted with the existing structure and system, but I suspect that these people would also be realistic enough to recognize that an organizational system as large as this does not change from without, but it does change from within. We all recognize that what we have is far from perfect; we also recognize that we are willing to change when the change proposed holds promise for increased productivity, better working conditions, and so on.

A Case of Mistaken Identity

Industrial arts education has frequently been mistaken for, or identified with, vocational industrial education. This is understandable, since students and teachers in both subject matter areas are directly involved with industry, and to the casual observer, the laboratory of each may well look like the others. The difference, of course, lies in the reason why each exists. The purposes of the two are completely different.

If we can remember that vocational industrial education is designed to prepare an individual to qualify for a skilled job in our market place and that industrial arts is designed to study that market place, much of the confusion about the two subject matter areas will no longer exist.

The Purpose of Industrial Arts

Let us imagine that we are going to study our industrial-technological society by placing a specimen of that society on a slide and then look at our specimen through a microscope and record our findings. Once the microscope is in focus, we can see that our industrial-technological society has:

1. workers with skills and knowledge
2. managers with skills and knowledge
3. buildings with equipment
4. energy—generation, distribution, control
5. raw materials: locating, extracting, processing, refining
6. production: materials handling, planning, quality control, cutting, shaping, forming
7. financing
8. marketing, sales, advertising
9. unions

We all recognize that to teach all these things is no small task. How have we accomplished this in the past? How are we doing it now? What should we do in the future?

Educational philosophers have long known that the more involved a student becomes in the learning process, the better he learns. And so we discovered the project. In the past—and also in the present—many industrial arts teachers have thought that by allowing their students to construct a project, all the things that we saw through our microscope would become crystal clear. These people believe in a kind of educational osmosis.

We know that this limited view of the project was and is doomed to failure. Yet in too many instances, the project, in its very limited and narrow sense, is all that is available for too many students in too many schools. Many of my colleagues in professional industrial arts education score me for my criticism of the project, and it is a criticism I do not accept. For I insist that we ought to view the project in its larger sense. The project should involve the marshaling of skills and technical information about a given part of our industrial-technological society so that every student will develop an appreciation for, and an understanding of, every major facet of that industry. If by means of lectures, student reports, outside readings, films, talks by visiting specialists, and other methods, students can integrate their projects into a comprehensive study about a particular part of our industrial-technological society, then the project will have reacquired its place in the educational scheme of things. I call for the development of concepts, problem-solving abilities, and a questioning, research-oriented point of view in our industrial arts laboratories.

We live in an age when strikes and the threat of strikes have become a standard part of our work-a-day world. Yet I have seldom seen an industrial arts teacher take time to study the problems of labor-management relations with his students. The carpenters in the community could be out on strike, and the industrial arts teacher could be a woods specialist—students (some possibly even sons and daughters of those on strike) could be designing and constructing projects of wood—wood which had been processed from the time the tree was selected to be harvested until the dressed material was delivered to the industrial arts laboratory by men who worked for wages and who belonged to unions. Some of that teacher's students could also be sons and daughters of the management team. Yet the thought seldom enters the industrial arts teacher's mind to get his students involved in studying the problems of labor unions, together with problems of management.

As I see it, the concepts which we wish to teach—on purpose—must be essential parts of any instructional activity in our industrial arts laboratories. Furthermore, if we would only talk about these issues and concepts, and not employ projects, we would lose the essential part of a proven method of effective instruction. This, in my opinion, would be just as bad as the industrial arts instructor who only says: "Let's go to work."

How Does One Become an Industrial Arts Teacher?

Industrial arts teachers receive their formal education at colleges and universities which offer majors in that field of study. Here in California, we have 19 state colleges, only nine of which offer industrial arts teacher preparation. Additionally, two private colleges offer this major. You should know, however, that at one time the University of California at Santa Barbara had one of the most outstanding industrial arts teacher preparation programs ever developed. This major was dropped several years ago when certain so-called academicians decided that this particular kind of preparation was not appropriate for a university.

In any event, students who enroll as industrial arts majors must meet the same admission requirements as any other major. They are in every respect fully qualified students. Each industrial arts major must meet the same graduation requirements as any other major on campus, including grade point average, general studies, upper division courses, and so on. At Chico State, we have perhaps made our program more rigorous than others by not only requiring substantial courses in mathematics, physics, and chemistry, but also courses in computer science, business administration, and economics.

145

Needless to say, the student's major in industrial arts is of paramount importance. A student majoring in industrial arts is required to complete several basic courses, each dealing with a significant industrial material, concept, or process. Typically, these courses are usually called "Basic Woods," "Fundamentals of Plastics," and "Introductory Electronics." As the student studies to complete these required or common courses, he also begins to complete a concentration or major area of emphasis. This major area of emphasis is usually descriptive of a job-family, or major sector of our industrial-technological society. Examples would be: "Machine-Tool," "Industrial Plastics," "Energy Conversion, Power, and Transportation," and "Electronics." Courses taken, skills acquired, technical information retained (with knowledge about the source of updated technical information in the future), and concepts developed would revolve around this major area of emphasis. Courses within the area of concentration are designed to build student skills and knowledge in an orderly, logical manner. In most first-class institutions of higher learning, the student is also required to complete a supporting area of study within the major—if the student's major area of concentration were machine tool, a likely supporting area of study would be drafting and design.

By law, most college students not only must complete a major but also must complete a minor. We at Chico State College recognize that student interest may be the determining factor in what that minor may be, but our faculty members encourage minors in business administration, mathematics, and the natural sciences.

We in higher education frequently get carried away with talking about classes, courses, units, requirements, and the like. You should know—and we should remember—that what we are talking about are learning opportunities, skills acquired, technical information assimilated, and problem-solving abilities developed.

In the past, instruction in college-university industrial arts classes had centered around students receiving technical-related information, observing demonstrations involving specific technical skills—practicing those skills under the watchful eye of the instructor—designing a project which would require the further development of the newly-acquired skills and technical information, and then constructing the project, bringing into play the full resources at his command, including the mass of intelligence acquired about the material or process being studied.

The only thing wrong with this entire system of instruction is that you people in industry no longer build things "one at a time." It is safe to say that conveyer-belt mass production changed that one-of-a-kind system just about the turn of the century.

So we in professional industrial arts teacher education have devised several "plans" for making our instruction more substantive. Recently, these have included the American Industries Plan at Stout State University, the Maryland Plan, Industriology, the Worlds of Manufacturing and Construction at Ohio, and certain others. The men who have initiated these plans are to be commended, for they have dared to break away from the comfortable, traditional way of running the railroad. At Chico State College, we have stressed these things:

1. Make the project a maximum rather than a minimum idea.
2. The development of concepts is more important than the mere acquisition of skills and technical information—both of which may and will become obsolete.
3. What a person learns is more important than what he makes.

I become concerned when a principal or some other visitor in an industrial arts laboratory asks a student, "What are you making?" This kind of question reveals a serious lack of comprehension of the fundamental purpose of the industrial arts program. His question ought to be—and if the question becomes pointed, so much the better—"What are you learning?"

As a college student approaches the completion of his four years of preparation, he is required to enroll in certain classes taught by those in education and psychology on how to teach and how we learn. These classes—termed education courses—have been under heavy fire from some quarters in recent years because some education courses have been devised with little content or value and, to top them off, have been themselves poorly taught. Properly taught, however, these courses can provide the teacher-to-be, and ultimately his students, with the methods, techniques, and confidence which should make teaching and learning a unique and joyful experience.

Student Teaching

Still closer to the end of his formal education, each industrial arts student is required to complete a semester of student teaching. The student is assigned to a specific master teacher in

147

a certain secondary school. Now, in effect, the master teacher should view this student teacher as his most troublesome charge, for if he does his job correctly, the student teacher will require the expenditure of additional time and energy—not less. In addition to his usual 25 to 30 secondary students, he now has another student with which to contend—one who asks stupid questions, makes mistakes, gets underfoot, gives out faulty information, and is a slow learner "to boot." Most master teachers will instruct the student teacher to observe how he teaches his classes, and to familiarize himself with the routines which are a necessary part of laboratory instruction. After classes, they will discuss the how and why of the day. The student teacher will be instructed to prepare a demonstration which will fit into the course of study prepared by the master teacher. This demonstration could be as simple as "How To Cut External Threads with a Die." At an appropriate time, the demonstration will be given by the student teacher. After the demonstration has been completed, the master teacher will have a critique-conference with the student teacher, where positive points will be praised and negative features will be described, together with ways and means for improving the latter. During the demonstration, however, the master teacher remains quiet, alert for detecting those things which he will call attention to during the conference.

Gradually, the student teacher assumes greater and greater responsibility for the conduct and management of the class, until one day the master teacher becomes only an observer.

We have just described the ideal. Too frequently, the master teacher sees the student teacher as a chance for some unofficial "released time," and no one profits from that kind of situation. The student teacher does not learn about deficiencies that need correcting, and the secondary students are possibly subjected to misinformation or, at best, poor instruction.

Who Can Teach?

After the student teacher has completed requirements for the A.B. degree and student teaching, he usually can begin teaching in a secondary school. Most states require that a person obtain a license to teach. In California, we call that license a credential. The credential has been equated with certain additional experiences and courses designed to add luster and polish to the novice and to allow the individual to become a professional teacher. In most states, this amounts to roughly one more year of college beyond the A.B. degree. By no small coincidence, most of these requirements closely parallel the requirements for an M.A. degree. In practice, credential course requirements are generally "additional depth" courses in an individual's major plus graduate courses designed to sharply focus the learner's awareness and skills in student achievement and evaluation, curriculum development, laboratory planning, analysis of instruction, and the like.

Most states permit an individual to begin teaching with a limited or partial license—generally with an A.B. degree plus student teaching. These individuals are then required to complete the credential requirements within a generous time line. Since most salary schedules are tied to credentials possessed and units acquired, individuals who begin their teaching with a partial license are generally eager to complete requirements for a full license.

Those of us in industrial arts teacher education—and those who hire our products—would like to see each graduate acquire some significant experience in the world of work before he begins his teaching career.

It is obvious that we in industrial arts teacher preparation have equated potential effective instruction with the A.B. degree, a strong major, one or more teaching minors, a credential or license, graduate study, and work experience. Insofar as the industrial arts profession as a whole is concerned, this appears to be a valid assumption. In far too many cases, however, individuals within the profession fall far short of this ideal.

The Secondary Industrial Arts Teacher

Our student teacher has now completed his assignment, been awarded the A.B. degree, earned a teaching credential, and is probably very close to an M.A. degree. The Waybelow Standard School District has notified his college placement office that a teaching vacancy exists in one of their high schools. Our hero applies for the position and is ultimately hired. What and how will he teach his students?

Industrial arts at the secondary level is much like industrial arts at the college-university level. You will recall that our teacher-specialist has received preparation in one interrelated materials-centered subject. It is reasonable to expect that the principal of the school to which our brand new teacher has been assigned will, in his infinite wisdom, be sure that the teaching assignment matches the teacher's preparation. Needless to say, this does not always happen.

149

The teacher will choose certain projects which the students will construct as they begin their study of a part of our industrial-technological society. The teacher will guide the learning activities so that the students will progress from the simple to the complex; he will carefully prepare demonstrations so that his students will learn the correct way to perform skills; he will assign outside study so that texts and journals will have to be devoured; he will assign individual reports so that students will acquire in-depth information about topics in which they are interested; he will administer written and performance examinations so that student achievement can be evaluated and his teaching performance checked; and he will so order his daily teaching that, when his courses have been completed, his students will have learned a great deal about a portion of their industrial-technological society. The students will have constructed projects along the way, but these projects represent focusing devices so that learning will be enhanced. The project has become a group of learning experiences.

One of the enduring values of industrial arts education is the individual and small-group instruction which can and does take place. After a group demonstration has been given, the wise industrial arts teacher will move about among his students giving individual instruction. It is at this time that mistakes can be corrected before they become bad habits.

Where Do Industrial Arts Education and Vocational Industrial Education Touch?

Inevitably, the question will be asked, "Can an industrial arts student get a job in industry?" The answer is "Yes," for many students obtain jobs in industry without ever being near an industrial arts laboratory. I suspect that the question being asked is: "Can a student who has studied industrial arts compete successfully in the job market with students who have followed a vocational industrial curriculum?" The answer to this question is "Yes and no." The industrial arts student will have a greater understanding of the entire industrial-technological society and how it operates than will the vocational industrial student, but the latter will initially have greater skill development.

It is obvious that we are speaking of an educational continuum. We know that education never stops. We also know that what is general education for one person may be special education for another. This is true because the way an individual decides to use acquired knowledge and skills will be the

150

sole determinant as to whether his education has been general or special. It is possible that information and knowledge and skills acquired by an individual will be used for purposes of general education at one time, and later as special education.

We in industrial arts should never lose sight of the fact that we teach and guide the learning processes of young people—and that learning is an exciting, individual adventure.

Conclusion

Various kinds of education have been devised by man to accomplish predetermined goals and objectives. In tracing the pattern of education, we have found that schools have been established to do that which parents had previously done. Some plausible reasons for this shift were enunciated, including man's penchant for specialization, the awesome impact of the industrial revolution, together with the factory system of conveyer belt mass production, and convenience. We have noted that education is either general or special, that the state can and does specify what must be taught at various levels, and that local boards of education can add other requirements for purposes of graduation.

We have noted that general education is frequently that education which is required in a given school, and that special education is largely elective. Examples of general education include English, physical education, and industrial arts; special education counterparts would be technical report writing, varsity athletics, and vocational industrial education. We have said that industrial arts is a study of the tools, materials, processes, successes, and failures of our industrial-technological society. Students who enroll in industrial arts classes generally construct projects. Major philosophical theories of education have been developed around the project and its usefulness as a positive teaching method. These theories break down only when individual industrial arts teachers lose sight of the larger goals and purposes of industrial arts. To assume that a student will learn about the complex metals industries of our society by constructing a project in metals is to be naive in the extreme. We have found that a carefully-prepared professional industrial arts teacher—hopefully with significant industrial experience—will select those things which he knows by analysis and experience to be valuable and then teach them on purpose—not by accident.

Finally, we need to recognize that professionals and laymen alike will at times confuse industrial arts education with vocational industrial education. If we remember our microscope, however, we will not have that problem in this forum—the student of industrial arts studies our industrial-technological society in its various parts and as a whole with almost a clinical point of view, so that he can understand how and why it works; the student of vocational industrial education studies how to become a competitive payroll worker in that society.

The Responsibility of Industrial Arts for Interpreting Technology

Donald Maley

My role on this program of the Mideast Forum for Man/Society/Technology is to focus on the responsibility of industrial arts for interpreting technology.

In the pursuit of the topic, I will carve out for you some of my biases, hopes, and perhaps some educational perspectives regarding the two elements—industrial arts and technology.

I am not so certain that each of you will identify what I am about to say with what is commonly known as industrial arts. Just as the summer changes to fall, and the Model "T" gave way to the more modern Ford, we in the last hundred years have moved from an agrarian society to an industrial society and more recently to a post-industrial or even super-industrial society. It is here in this latter development that I find the new challenge to what we have commonly called industrial arts. The changing society has made it possible for less than 6% of our people to produce enough food to feed our own population, as well as another comparable population scattered throughout the world. We have witnessed an ever-increasing industrial productivity with a constantly decreasing percentage of people needed to produce it. The year 1956 is credited with being the point in time when the white-collar workers outnumbered the blue-collar workers, and it has been predicted that by 1985 we will be able to produce all of our material goods with 3% of the population (2, p. 90). This trend is in the main a factor of technology. Thus, there is some doubt in my mind whether, if we hold to the concept of general education as that form of education designed for all persons, we can insist on a program that derives its content from the efforts of so few in the society.

It is here that I would make my bid for the emphasis on the study of technology. I would not limit such a study to the technology of industry or production. Nor would I advocate, for general education purposes, the in-depth, taxonomical study of any one or more of the identifiable technologies.

My reasoning in this regard is not geared to the study of technology as a function of one's employment, but in a much broader sense—I would opt for a study of technology that would be useful to the future citizen of a democratic nation as he tries to solve the pressing problems of his society.

Man has forged for himself a technological capability that extends his intellectual and physical potential into every facet of his existence—that is, of course, if man understands the options it lays open for him.

The cult of ignorance that prevails in a society possessed of untapped technological "know-how" and a society of vast **wealth is clearly apparent when the people of that society have insufficient electrical power, inadequate transportation systems, sub-standard housing in abundance, sprawling urban centers that cry out for every conceivable form of human need, sprawling junk yards that endlessly clutter our country-side, polluted air and contaminated water—yes, and a seeming depletion of fresh water sources, as well as a reckless waste of natural resources on every hand. The ignorance referred to is not a matter of technological development or even technological capability. It is largely a problem of societal ignorance and societal indifference to technological applications similar to that of the antiquated farmer who holds fast to his wooden plow.**

I will base my argument for the study of technology and its interpretation on the "need to know" and the "need to understand" on the part of the individual as a functionary within the democratic framework. You will notice that I have taken just one element of a whole range of potential human interactions with technology in the society of the present and future.

Time here this evening does not permit an exploration of the implications of the study of technology as it relates to career planning, leisure activities, consumer participation, or other vital forms of human interaction with this important phenomenon. But here again, I am confident that industrial arts or some other appropriate title can and must play an important role with each of the areas listed.

I will pick out as my piece of the pie that portion which relates to the individual as a voting member and a participant in the democratic processes, and one who will share in the shaping of tomorrow. Specifically, I would like to emphasize the application of technology in the solution of major problems facing mankind in the future.

Here the rank and file of our democratic society come face to face with the problem at the voting booth, in community meetings, in planning and zoning hearings, and in the mass demonstrations we have come to know so well.

To further delineate the role of industrial arts in the study of technology, the following major problem areas fit within the topic as well as within the realm of feasibility.

pollution	conservation
power generation	more effective resource utilization
housing	trash and waste disposal
transportation	industrial productivity
communication	

There are many other problem areas that plague this society as well as future societies, such as health, poverty, social inequities, economics, etc. No one area of the school can deal effectively in the total range of man's problems. However, experimental programs in industrial arts have demonstrated the appropriateness of the selected problem areas previously mentioned. Such programs are highly interdisciplinary in their operation and processes.

The charge to industrial arts is not to develop the solutions, although this does present some interesting possibilities. The major function would be one of education. That is, the education of the citizenry regarding technological developments that are or may be capable of solving the problems of pollution, housing, transportation, power generation, etc.

This point is reinforced by an excellent statement in *The Dynamics of Change* which reads as follows.

> The contention that persons ignorant of technology can function in a democracy to any affect when the society is a technological one is dubious. Understanding is not a prerequisite of control, it is control (3, p. 30).

The great need is for an interpretation of technology so that intelligent decisions can be made at all levels in society. Major debates are presently being conducted in numerous localities regarding the development of nuclear power generating stations, pollution control measures, conservation projects, housing, transportation needs, and many more.

Decision making in a democracy demands levels of understanding that frequently have not been available or sufficiently developed. Classic examples in our own history include the burning and destruction of the early looms, a technological development that would one day make possible the clothing of hundreds of millions of people. The destruction of the early cotton gins is another example of technological ignorance. Perhaps the most classic example was the prolonged and bitter strikes that accompanied the installation of automatic dialing facilities in the telephone system. The volume of calls on any ordinary day is so great that it would be utterly impossible to find enough operators available to handle a fraction of the load. The history of mankind is filled with instances of technological ignorance that delayed progress and of instances when progress was won after bitter conflict, strife, strikes, and human loss.

Permit me to give you a few examples of the present potential open to mankind through the fruits of technology.

"Dr. Lee A. DuBridge, President of the California Institute of Technology, has said that, from a purely technical standpoint, we now know enough to:

1. Produce enough food to feed every mouth on earth—and to do this even though the population may double or triple.

2. Make fresh water out of sea water and then irrigate all of the world's arid regions.

3. Produce enough energy from uranium to light and heat our homes and offices, electrify our railroads, and run our factories and mills.

4. Build houses, buildings, and indeed whole cities, which are essentially waterproof, heatproof, cold proof, and storm proof" (1, p. 13).

Dr. Alvin W. Weinberg, Director of the Oak Ridge National Laboratories, has made some interesting observations in an article titled: "Can Technology Replace 'Social Engineering'?" (13, p. 56, 57).

Dr. Weinberg identified two past technological fixes on social problems that have plagued man for centuries: war and widespread poverty. It is Dr. Weinberg's idea that

> Edward Teller may have supplied the nearest thing to a quick technological fix to the problem of war. The hydrogen bomb greatly increases the provocation necessary to lead to large scale war....

Secondly, a technological fix was made on widespread poverty through the use of technology in the greatly expanded production system involving mass production and automation.

A third social problem that Dr. Weinberg speculates on with respect to a technological fix is the great water shortages experienced in such areas as Southern California and the Eastern Seaboard. This would involve the use of nuclear desalination plants. It is estimated that water costs would be less than ten cents per thousand gallons. This would depend upon the development of inexpensive electrical power from huge nuclear reactors.

John McHale in his text, *The Future of the Future*, put it this way:

> Our chances of survival are clearly based on our capacity to meet the largest challenge ever offered to man. Technologies and 'know-how' are more than adequate to solve many of our largest problems. What we lack is that combination of vision, understanding, and innovative action that will enable us to use our knowledge more immediately and more effectively (7, p. 170).

The thrust of this new form of industrial arts would be aimed at another important problem that faces mankind in the present and certainly will more so in the future.

The problem is an ever-widening gap between the technologist (the technical elite) and the great masses of people who use or must make decisions about the application, acceptance, or rejection of that technology.

Walter W. Finke has indicated that:

> A language barrier as real as any that exists in the world today separates the technocratic society from the remainder of society. And the tragedy is that little attempt is made to break down the barrier... (4, p. 49).

The gap between the technologist and the populace in general was a concern of Sir Charles Snow when he said:

> ...that he feared that technological progress would eventually lead to a situation in which life-or-death decisions would one day

be made by a small scientific elite "who do not quite understand the depth of the argument."

This is, he said, "one of the consequences of the lapse or gulf in communication between scientists and nonscientists" (4, p. 50).

A similar concern was expressed by Barbara Ward in her text *Spaceship Earth*, in which there is a concern for the impact of technology and the control of political and economic policy.

In a world that is being driven onward at apocalyptic speed by science and technology, we cannot, we must not, give up the idea that human beings can control their political and economic policies... (12, p. 1).

Perhaps an even more pointed element was contained in the report from the Commission on the Year 2000. The report projected:

The end of democratic government as people lose interest and leave the decisions to an intellectual, technological elite (10, p. F-1).

The solution for each of these concerns lies in the nature of education that is a part of each individual's program. I am suggesting that to not have a significant emphasis on the role of technology in society as a part of general education would indeed be walking directly into the pitfalls so identified by the Commission on the Year 2000, Sir Charles Snow, Walter Finke, and Barbara Ward.

The need for greater emphasis on the role of technology and its part in the evolving social scene is highlighted by the factor of time. In many instances, it may more appropriately be called lead time.

The acceleration of technological innovation and the ensuing accelerated changes in society have contributed to major social, economic, and psychological problems.

The time to adjust and span of time for adjustment are crucial matters. The slow-moving dynamics of technology as experienced by those living in the previous centuries allowed considerable time for adjustment and assimilation. However, the present and the future are marked by a protraction of time, with predictions for the future of even greater acceleration.

Let us examine a few examples. From the moment of scientific invention until the manufacture of the product, the time lag was as follows for the items below (Ref. 9).

158

112 years for photography (1727-1839)
 56 years for the telephone (1820-1876)
 35 years for the radio (1867-1902)
 15 years for radar (1925-1940)
 12 years for television (1922-1934)
  6 years for the atomic bomb (1939-1945)
  5 years for the transistor (1948-1953)
  3 years for the integrated circuit (1958-1961)

The same kind of an analysis can be made with equal or even more accelerated projections in the fields of medicine, speed of travel, production, construction, metallurgy, and many more. A graphic plot of such technological accleration is presented in Figure 1.

The resultant takes on many dimensions, such as the increasing reduction of the half-life of the engineer; the need for new plants and equipment; the altering of accepted social values; the concept of planned obsolescence; the protracting of time and distance; the widening impact of individual or group activities; the knowledge explosion; and many more.

The significance of the study of the role of technology in this accelerated pace is that it would equip the individual with the capability to anticipate certain changes and to have in some instances evaluated alternatives. It also is anticipated that such a study of the influence of technology on man's future problems would provide a higher tolerance for change as one sees the contributing elements grow, emerge, or come to pass.

It does present an interesting hypothesis that those who study the future problems and the associated accelerating technological developments would be in less conflict with the changes that come about than would the individual who did not engage in such study and concentrated on the past.

I am in essence pleading the case for a form of education that looks to the future for its direction and relevance.

The development of such a program aimed at the interpretation of technology at the senior high school level would in deed and fact place the student in a position he has sought. We have heard the cries for "relevance," "appropriateness," "pertinence." We have heard the cries of students for involvement in shaping the world they have inherited. We have heard the cries of students who seek to remedy the ills of society. And recently we have given them the right to vote in our local, state, and national elections. A major tool in the accomplishing of the needs which they (the students) and the older generation seek is available to both of us. But education is the missing link that is needed to complete the triangle. It is a kind of education that explores the options to mankind as it tackles the problems of a society whose population will double in 30 years.

This point was emphasized by Fred Wilhelms in an article entitled: "Which Way to a Curriculum for Adolescents."

> Yet, even more fundamentally, all youth of our day are growing into an age of uncertainty about themselves and about their significance ... They are threshing about, often in crudely rebellious or even bizarre ways; but the important thing is that they are searching, impelled by a fine idealism and relentless honesty. They deserve our help. And to give it to them we shall have to shuck off a lot of scholastic impediments and go to where a young person meets the realities of adulthood (14, p. 15).

It is obviously clear that a senior high school industrial arts program which attempts to deal with the applications of technology in the solution of major societal problems should be broad-based and relevant to the total spectrum of students, as opposed to present offerings that favor limited skill and technical development. It is projected that such a program would assume the dimension of inclusiveness that would not be hemmed in by occupational aspiration or curricular involvement. The problems as identified belong to no special group. They are everybody's problem.

The objective is to arrive at a content that is integrally tied with major societal problems to such an extent that the school would actually move out into the mainstream of life itself. It is to be an educational program that explores the solutions of man's pressing problems, present and future. The student will in this way find himself a part of the on-going scene. This principle of contemporary involvement is supported in a statement by Arthur W. Foshay in an article appearing in the March 1970 issue of *Phi Delta Kappan.*

> Our secondary school students ... want to see themselves as participants in the world they live in, not as apprentices for it. They want the world to be in the school and the school in the world (5, p. 352).

Here the issue of relevancy comes into play. The population is a fast-maturing high school student body with a sophistication that far exceeds its predecessors. Today's student is greatly concerned about where society is going and what lies ahead. The communication media of television, radio, newspapers, and paperbacks have continuously bombarded the student with endless commentary on each of the problem

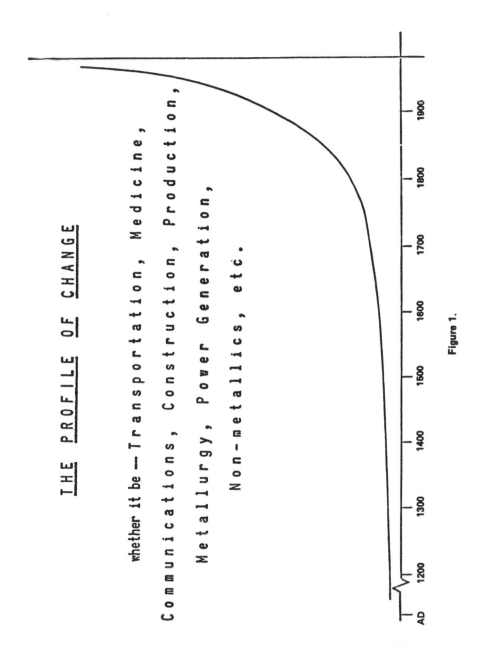

Figure 1.

161

areas identified for study. The central concerns of this program are in fact central concerns of society itself. This in itself is a profound difference over the content of present and past programs. Other educators have expressed similar interest in dealing with contemporary social and environmental problems.

Dr. John Goodlad, in an article titled "The Educational Program to 1980 and Beyond," has urged a look ahead in curriculum development.

> ...Get into the curriculum the problems likely to be facing young adults in 1980. These persons currently are in the primary years of schooling. If we were to begin now, we could plan for them a junior high school curriculum organized around problems of population, poverty, pollution, and many more (6, p. 57).

Another objective of the high school program is to place the student and the industrial arts activity out in the mainstream of life. This will involve a whole new orientation on the part of the teacher, as well as the school itself.

Ralph Tyler, in a discussion of the "Curriculum for A Troubled Society," has stated that

> One factor standing in the way of developing an effective curriculum and educational program is the tradition that the high school should be an adolescent island outside the major currents of adult life (11, p. 35).

The involvement of the student in the examination of the problems of pollution, power generation, housing, transportation, etc., the study of alternate solutions, and the identification of future problems could have profound effects upon the future. I will venture to mention a few as follows:

1. The voting public (decision makers) of the future would have a sensitivity to the kind, nature, and extent of such problems facing mankind.

2. The student would have some understanding of and sensitivity to the nature of solutions and the alternatives related to the problem.

3. The strength of his adult participation in dealing with such problems may be greatly enhanced by his earlier involvement in real and direct experiences related to them.

4. The student, through appropriate kinds and levels of involvement, could begin to feel he is a part of the system and he does have a role to play.

5. The student's communication with his or her parents and other adults on the concerns and activities of the program would have the potential for even wider levels of involvement.

But now you must be asking the question—"Why this role for industrial arts?" I will venture the following.

1. It is one of the very few areas in the school that deals with technology and principally applied technology.

2. The program as projected would include a great deal of construction, design, evaluation, and expression opportunities that could be carried on in the well-equipped present laboratories.

3. The discipline-centered areas in the school tend to focus on building the student's strength in the discipline and give little concern for its application on broad-based problems.

4. The "interaction with the community" phase of the program closely parallels many activities already in the better industrial arts programs.

5. The program would require a high degree of inter-disciplinary involvement with most other areas of the school and community, and industrial arts teachers have the laboratories and the training necessary to carry it out.

6. It is in some regard an imperative for industrial arts in pursuing its past emphasis on industry and technology. That is to say, the future is increasingly dependent upon the role of technology, and industrial arts is obligated to keep in step.

7. From a practical point of view, a small number of industrial arts teachers have already demonstrated the feasibility of such a program.

I do not mean to imply that industrial arts alone has a corner on the market for the interpretation of technology or even its application to societal problems. There appears to be enough work and problems for all to share.

The role of any area of the school is pertinent to the extent that it has made two important decisions. To what extent does the area develop a sensitivity to the changes in society and as a result acquire a vibrant harmony with the society it serves? To what extent does the area project itself into the future so that the problems of a future generation may be tempered by a previous generation that has dared to examine the alternatives?

In the course of this presentation, I have attempted to present a position as well as a projected program relative to a role for industrial arts in the interpretation of technology.

I have developed brief sketches of rationale to support such a position as well as the projected programs.

In the process, I have made a plea for a kind of education that starts with the present and extends into the future, as well as indicating the vital part industrial arts can play.

I have attempted to portray a new role for the school and industrial arts in particular in which there would be a move from the traditional emphasis on passive involvement with the past to an aggressive excitement and active encounter with the future. This latter involvement with the future was identified by C.P. Snow as a matter of greatest need for man when he stated:

> ...We can no longer afford the kind of formalized education which takes the child into the future with his gaze fixed steadfastly on the past. Somehow we must convince our patrons that it is more important to help the child to think about the next civilization that to require him to remember the facts of the last one (8, p. 24).

It is my contention that industrial arts has a very significant role to play in this process.

Literature Cited

1. Bernado, James V. "Educational Implications of the Space Program." *Apogee 67,* second quarter (published quarterly by the Douglass Aircraft Co.) May 1967.
2. Colm, Gerhard. "Prospective Economic Developments," *Prospective Changes in Society By 1980.* Denver: Bradford-Robinson Co., July 1966.
3. Fabun, Don. *The Dynamics of Change.* New Jersey: Prentice-Hall, Inc., 1968, p. 170 (Chapter 1).
4. Finke, Walter W. "Making Technology a Universally Available Tool," *Space Digest,* January 1967.
5. Foshay, Arthur W. "How Fare the Disciplines?" *Phi Delta Kappan,* Volume LI, No. 7 (March 1970) p. 352.
6. Goodlad, John I. "The Educational Program to 1980 and Beyond," *Implications for Education of Prospective Changes in Society.* E.L. Morphet and C.O. Ryan, Ed. New York: Citation Press, 1967, p. 57.
7. McHale, John. *The Future of the Future.* New York: George Braziller, 1969, p. 322.
8. Rubin, Louis H. "The Object of Schooling: An Evolutionary View," *Life Skills in School and Society.* ASCD Yearbook, Washington, D.C.: National Education Association, 1969, p. 171.
9. Servan-Schreiber, Jean Jacques. *The American Challenge.* New York: Athenum, 1968, p. 291.

10. Squibb, Andrew. "The Year 2000: What Will Life Be Like?" (Part One), *The News American.* Baltimore, Maryland. Sunday, January 14, 1968.

11. Tyler, Ralph W. "Curriculum for a Troubled Society," *NCEA Bulletin.* Volume 66, No. 1 (August 1969) p. 35.

12. Ward, Barbara. *Spaceship Earth.* New York: Columbia University Press, 1966.

13. Weinberg, Alvin M. "Can Technology Replace 'Social Engineering'?" *Space Digest.* January 1967.

14. Wilhelms, Fred T. "Which Way to a Curriculum for Adolescents," *NEA Journal* (December 1967) pp. 13-15.

JOHN DEWEY

V.S.

THE SOCIAL EFFICIENCY

PHILOSOPHERS[1]

Arthur G. Wirth

The subject of industrial or vocational education was the most controversial matter confronting school men as we came into the twentieth century. A new America had come into being—an America transformed by science and marked by technology, corporatism, and urbanism. To continue with an educational system unresponsive to such realities was intolerable.

Meetings of educators were filled with speeches on the topic of vocationalism, and educational philosophers were forced to confront questions raised in the debates. Powerful interest groups like the National Association of Manufacturers, the American Federation of Labor, farm organizations, and settlement house leaders moved in to take positions. A closer look at the debate that raged for nearly two decades prior to enactment of Smith-Hughes (1917) shows that more than educational policy questions were involved: at issue was the question of what quality American culture would assume under conditions of technology and metropolitanism. The bedrock question was whether Americans would find it possible to create a social order which could combine technological efficiency with humane, democratic values and traditions.

Two educational philosophies emerged which probed the value issues and articulated sharply differing policy recommendations: the social efficiency philosophy of David Snedden and Charles Prosser[2] and the experimentalism of John Dewey. The purpose of this paper is to make a brief comparison of some salient features of the two philosophies. The thesis is that the issues considered in the first round of the vocational-liberal studies debate are still very much alive as we approach the last quarter of the twentieth century.

Dewey and the social efficiency philosophers both agreed that traditional schooling was failing in urban America. Compulsory school attendance laws confined children in classrooms for years of verbal recitations on dull, standardized textbooks. The school and its youthful population were "isolated from life." Children chafed under classroom conditions which denied them the chance to explore and actively discover the contours of the real world. They fled school in large numbers, despite endless administrative efforts to induce them to stay.

Both philosophies agreed that vocationalism as affected by science and technology ought to play a prominent role in a reformed education. Their conception of the form that vocationalism should take, however, and their ideas of how it should be related to the larger society, differed sharply.

Pedagogically, Snedden and Prosser articulated the position that a straight-forward set of specific skill training programs should be added as an overlay to academic studies. Such a curriculum would be offered at the point which preceded the student's entry into work. The content of training programs would be derived from a study of the needs of industry.

To Snedden and Prosser, it seemed apparent that the way for all Americans to serve their own best interests was to re-tool public schools to meet the needs of the nation's fabulously productive economic machine. The social efficiency philosophy assumed that the goals of increased productivity, material wealth, and social power represented the culmination of human well-being. In this view, Snedden and Prosser were merely expressing one of the major articles of faith of the American people. As Samuel Hays observed in his comments on life in the U.S.A. in 1914,

> The American people subordinated religion, education, and politics to the process of creating wealth. Increasing production, employment, and income became the measure of community success, and personal riches the mark of individual achievement.[3]

It must be acknowledged, however, that vocational leaders like Charles Prosser spoke to a real and important problem. They had the imagination and energy to develop the rationale for manpower training programs to replace the out-dated apprenticeship tradition. They brought into the open a set of complex and critically important questions: Which training programs should be offered? By whom? For whom? At what levels and for what age groups? Such questions are essential to the functioning of the technological society; they must be faced constantly and answered anew as this era unfolds.

The weakness of the early proponents of vocational education was the narrowness of their vision. They wanted to rule out most considerations other than the development of efficient training programs. They defined themselves so that they primarily were trainers rather than educators. This led them to miss the significance of the underlying revolution in science and technology that was transforming life and prevented them from seeing the potential use of technological and vocational studies to bring reform and relevance to general education.

The passion for practicality of the early vocationalists ultimately flawed even their conceptions of vocational training. Prosser's style of designing training programs to meet specific industrial needs was reflected in the features of the Smith-Hughes law and the mode of administering it. His insistence on detailed prescriptions handicapped vocational education from attaining the flexibility required to meet the demands of fast-moving technical and social change. Vocational education became marked by a quality of separatism as its leaders remained suspicious of collaboration with general educators. Parochial attitudes resulted, and vocational experiences tended to be limited to young people headed for immediate employment in industry. Federal legislation was drawn so that mainly narrow vocational training could be funded; experiments aimed at effecting interesting integrations between liberal and vocational studies were excluded.

John Dewey, the foremost educational philosopher of the time, brought a different perspective to the debate. He had relatively little to say on the question of how to develop effective manpower training programs, a matter which dominated the attention of the vocationalists.

He was motivated by another concern—that the quality of human experience was being changed by the advent of science, technology, corporate-industrialism, and urbanism, and that these developments contained potentials for debasing and dehumanizing life and for undermining the ideals of the demo-

168

cratic dream. He was convinced that only the most far-reaching economic, social, and educational reform could turn these trends toward human good. Dewey took on the task of delineating what he thought was the nature of the modern challenge: what the dangers were and what was needed in the way of institutional reconstruction. He took the position that major philosophical questions were at issue "in discussion of the proper place and function of vocational factors in education." Dewey saw, for example, the strong temptation of Americans to copy the German technocratic system, which chose unquestioningly to put schooling at the service of material gain and national power. He joined those who chose to resist such moves. He also rejected the position of those intellectuals who viewed science and technology as intrinsically alien to humane values.

A distinctive feature of Dewey's philosophy was his conviction that cultural renewal could be engendered from within the very system of science and technology which threatened men. Since he thought that necessary institutional change depended on man's developing new insights and attitudes, he assigned a pivotal role to education. His ambitious plan was to employ an interpretation of science, together with a reconstituted view of vocation, as the means for a general reform of education.

Dewey differed from those who insisted that science and technology lead inevitably to dehumanization and estrangement, because he saw scientific thought as part of an evolving human experience. Scientific thinking was a form of learning which had grown out of the history of man's interaction with the world. It was a form of learning which had enabled men to reconstruct and extend their understanding of nature and of themselves. Dewey also assumed that the attitudes and habits intrinsic to scientific inquiry could be generalized and made available to men everywhere: the habits of thinking hypothetically, of testing conjectures against experience, of freely exchanging results and conclusions, of creating communities tolerant of maverick ideas and life-styles as prerequisites to further insights and growths. In short, Dewey found congruence between the values of the scientific community and those cherished by the democratic tradition. This position might seem hopelessly dated and naive to many as they witness the deep disillusionment with and violent rejection of science and technology by influential intellectuals and the young of radical persuasion.

The fact that Dewey's interpretation of the positive possibilities of science can still be convincing to humanistic educators is illustrated by comments on Dewey by George Dennison, a pioneer in the modern Free School movement.

> Dewey stressed again and again . . . that it was not the external procedures of empirical science that needed to be adopted, but the dynamics between science and experience. Science organizes experience in a unique, and uniquely imitable, way. It cannot afford rigidity, or merely rhetorical reverence, yet it builds upon the past. It is instrumental, wholly alive to the present, yet it is open to the future and is no enemy of change. Free thought is its essence, yet it is disciplined by its devotion to emergent meaning. It places the highest value upon ideas, cannot function without them, defines them scrupulously, yet never enshrines them into final truths. It is always collaborative. Egotism, vanity, the power lusts of the individual will—all these are chastened by the authority of truth and the demonstrable structure of the natural world. These were the attributes Dewey cited in proposing empirical science as a model for the social effort we call education.[4]

And Paul Goodman in 1969 called for a social reformation in which our institutions would "return to the pure faith"—to the authentic values of science—prudence as to consequences, ecological concern, and decentralized modes of work and community living. He reminded his readers that it was on such values that "John Dewey devised a system of education to rear pragmatic and experimental citizens to be at home in the new technological world rather than estranged from it."[5]

In order to make the theoretical model operational, Dewey drew upon the concept of vocation. He saw possibilities for changing the dynamics of school practice through imaginative use of "the vocational aspects of education." The idea of establishing connections between the concepts of science and of vocation still seems strange. But Dewey's effort is understandable if we note his commitment to an evolutionary view of human experience. In this view, men were related to the rest of nature through their work—through their basic patterns of producing what was required for survival and growth. As Dewey saw it, each change in the mode of production or work-form led to transformations in the total patterns of culture. It was through vocations that men engaged in their basic interaction with nature and with each other. Thought, feeling,

170

and action were combined in vocations, and patterns of human relations and communication were established. Theory was wedded to practice in the mechanical and social techniques developed to get the work of the world done. The new education which Dewey projected was to be permeated with humane conceptions of science and vocation.

In actuality, public education repudiated both the educational approach recommended by John Dewey and the policies of social efficiency urged by Snedden and Prosser. The nation produced as a compromise the comprehensive secondary school which promised both to preserve the egalitarian values of the common school tradition and to satisfy the skill requirements of industrialism. But the actual performance of the schools demonstrated the strength of the pressures of the technocratic system. The use of ability tracks and differentiated courses tended to reflect and preserve the social class ordering of society. Prosser's kind of vocationalism isolated vocational training from academic courses. Imaginative integrations of liberal with vocational studies which might have served to enliven each were not effected. Students in "voc. ed." tended to move in a world separate from classmates headed for the university.

Technology has flourished in America for more than half a century since the passage of Smith-Hughes. Yet as we approach the bicentennial anniversary of the republic, we appear to be on the verge of social breakdown. In spite of a largely successful quest for material gain, Americans have failed to demonstrate that they can create a humane social order. Technological waste poisons the environment. Sensibilities are violated by the visual ugliness of our communities and by the cheap deceits of the advertising industry. Racist hatreds erupt into social conflict. Bitter differences over involvement in foreign wars alienate youth from their elders. In the major cities, more than half of all secondary-age students still choose to leave before completing high school. Disaffection has spread to the young of the suburbs, who question the life-style of their parents. In their confusion, the youth pathetically turn for relief to drugs or to strange cults of the irrational. Their hunger is for a civilization which is worthy of allegiance.

The compelling question of our time remains whether it will be possible to humanize life under technological conditions: whether democratic traditions of responsible participation can be re-vitalized, and whether individuals can attain a sense of personal meaning under conditions of the urban-industrial society.

171

Evidence of our willingness to re-order priorities will be revealed in ideas we generate for the education of our children. The temptation to proceed by seeking greater efficiency through a technocratic model, adding a variety of well-financed manpower training programs to traditional school studies, will remain strong. Such approaches enable us to stay within established routines and to fulfill the skill needs of industry and business. One of the critical tests of our intentions will be our answer to an important federal policy question: Will federal funding be limited to vocational training in the narrower sense, or will it be broadened and extended to include experiments and practice at all levels in which imaginative use is made of the "vocational aspects" of study in relation to general or liberal education?

The latter approach, in the Deweyan tradition, might indicate that we are ready to scrutinize the quality of our social life in terms of our espoused humane-democratic traditions To believe that the answers to our educational problems can be found intact in Dewey's philosophy is absurd. There is no single answer available to us now, and we would be better off if we gave up the search for one. We ought to take seriously the advice to "let a thousand flowers bloom." What can be said with confidence is that Dewey's thought was the most serious American philosophical effort to establish humanistic connections between education, science, and technology, and the democratic ideal. It might be fruitful once again to reflect upon this part of our intellectual heritage.

---

[1] This article is based on a chapter of a forthcoming book: Arthur G. Wirth, *Education In The Technological Society: The Vocational-Liberal Studies Debate In The Early Twentieth Century*. Scranton: intext Educational Publishers, 1971.

[2] David Snedden was Commissioner of Education in Massachusetts (1909-1916) when vocational education was introduced on the recommendation of a commission appointed by Governor Douglas (1906). Snedden later became a founder of the new discipline of educational sociology while professor at Teachers College, Columbia University. Charles A. Prosser was Executive Secretary of the National Society for the Promotion of Industrial Education (1912-1917) and the effective author of the Smith-Hughes Act.

[3] Samuel P. Hays, *The Response to Industrialism* (Chicago: The University of Chicago Press, 1965), p. 12.

[4] George Dennison, *The Lives of Children* (New York: Random House, 1969), page 248.

[5] Paul Goodman, "Can Technology be Humane," *The New York Review*, Nov. 20, 1969, pp. 27-34.

INDUSTRIAL EDUCATORS IN SWEDEN: THEIR STATUS AND THEIR EDUCATION

by

Kenneth S. Hansson

Industrial Education in Sweden has during the two decades since World War II undergone change at every level from the moderate evolution of sloyd to the rapid growth and revolution in vocational education and the completely new technical schools and programs. The teachers of these changing, expanding, and new programs have come from various sources and they have undergone various kinds of educational experiences before they became teachers. This paper will attempt to describe the duties, responsibilities, characteristics, and education of teachers in sloyd, trade, industrial, and technical subjects.

Status of Teachers in Sweden

Teachers in Sweden have for a long time enjoyed a rather secure position both economically and socially. Teachers of both academic subjects and practical subjects are held in high esteem by the people. The university professor is a prestige figure, and the highest posts in Government are often held by former professors. The present Prime Minister is a former professor. Teachers of practical subjects, however, do not enjoy as much prestige as teachers of academic subjects. Even so, the position of sloyd and vocational teacher are sought by many more than can be accepted or are needed.

Teachers in Sweden are generally classified into four basic groups: (1) classroom teachers for the self-contained classrooms in the lower and middle departments of the "grundskola," (2) subject matter teachers in specific subject matter fields, (3) art, music, physical education, and sloyd teachers (ovning-slarare), and (4) vocational teachers. Classroom teachers receive their specialized teacher education in teacher training institutions called "seminarier," while the subject matter teachers have additional work in universities. Art, music, physical education, and sloyd teachers receive their teacher education in special schools.

Most teachers in Sweden are employed on a permanent basis after a probationary period of approximately two years. Substitute and part-time teachers, who are paid hourly wages, are also employed. These teachers are often new teachers, or specialists from industry who teach specialized subjects in addition to their regular work.

In order to receive a permanent appointment, teachers must meet certain requirements as to health, teaching ability, education, teaching experience, and in the case of vocational teachers, practical work experience. Teachers on probation are employed as salaried non-permanent teachers or as full-time or part-time teachers paid an hourly wage. After a certain period of time in a non-permanent position, teachers may seek appointments to a semi-permanent position. Teachers who have a permanent appointment are paid a yearly salary. (10, pp. 1120, 1124).

In order to evaluate qualifications of teachers when they seek permanent positions, a merit rating system has been devised. The system is not employed to determine salaries of teachers since this is largely determined by the type of appointment, i.e. permanent, semi-permanent, and the type of school and teaching assignment. The three basic areas included in awarding points on the merit scale are (1) teachng skill and zeal of performance, (2) knowledge and skill which bear upon the teaching, and (3) time in teaching or in a related occupation in the case of vocational teachers. A rather involved point system has been developed which awards points for jobs, grades in teacher institutions, kind of course work, teaching experience, and various other activities and personal characteristics. (3, pp. 410-414).

Sloyd Teachers

Sloyd teachers instruct in wood and metal sloyd in the nine-year compulsory "grundskola," in the secondary "fackskola," in folk high schools, and in certain special types of schools and programs. Teachers in textile sloyd are not usually referred to a sloyd teachers but rather as textile, weaving, or sewing teachers. The great majority of sloyd teachers are men, while teachers of textile sloyd are, almost without exception, women.

Sloyd teachers in the past have been elementary (folkskola) teacher who had received sloyd training at Naas or some other sloyd training institute. The younger sloyd teachers are, in general, graduates of the "grundskola," a vocaitonal school, and the Sloyd Teachers Institute (sloyd-seminariet) in Linkoping, Sweden.

In order to become a sloyd teacher a person must meet the normal requirements such as being of good character and free from sickness and handicap which might impair teaching effectiveness. A future sloyd teacher must furthermore show ability to teach and a thorough knowledge of the subject matter. A sloyd teacher must also have passed the sloyd teacher's examination. In order to receive a permanent appointment the sloyd teacher must have taught sloyd successfully for at least 600 hours and taken the sloyd teacher's examination at least two years prior to the appointment. (11, pp. 1269-2170). The examination for sloyd teacher competency is taken upon completion of the course at the Sloyd Teachers Institute.

Sloyd teachers are required to teach thirty periods per week in the "grundskola." They may also be required to teach four additional periods for which they receive extra compensation. Sloyd teachers may, if qualified, teach vocational courses, but they must teach more than eight periods in sloyd and at least an equal number of periods in the vocational subject. Sloyd teachers may also, if qualified and with the permission of the National Board of Education, teach other classes. (11, p. 1267).

Permanent teachers in sloyd are appointed by the county educational boards (lansskolnamnderna) upon the recommendation of the local school board. All non-permanent teachers are appointed by the local school board. (10, p. 1158).

Evaluation of sloyd teachers for the purpose of filling permanent positions is based largely on the system of merits previously mentioned. In the category of teaching ability the applicant's grade (from one to three) in teaching skill is multiplied by twelve and weighs most heavily on the total score. The numerical grades of the general education subjects are added, and the course grades in design, psychology, and teaching methods are multiplied by four. Two points are added for the "folkskola" teacher's degree, and from one to three points for certain refresher courses. Points for length of teaching service are computed by multiplying by two each of the first ten years as a sloyd teacher. After the tenth year the multiplication factor decreases until it is 0.02 for the twentieth year and zero thereafter. The maximum number of points allowed for teaching experience is thirty. Although this system is far from perfect, it is considered better than no system at all since it provides a certain objective measure of a teacher's accomplishments. (3, pp. 410-414, 430-435).

The Sloyd Teacher's Education

With the opening in 1960 of the Sloyd Teachers Institute in Linkoping in the province of Ostergotland, a new era in sloyd teacher education began. Up to 1960 most sloyd teachers were "folkskola" teachers who had received six weeks of sloyd instruction at Naas or in other institutes. With the establishment of the Institute in Linkoping the courses at Naas became obsolete, and the last course was held during the summer of 1966.

The purpose of the Sloyd Teachers Institute, as stated by the legal statues under which it operates, is to prepare sloyd teachers in wood and metal sloyd and comparable kinds of sloyd. Both men and women are eligible for admission. (12, p. 1323).

The course is of forty-one weeks duration, of which twenty weeks constitute the fall semester and twenty-one weeks the spring semester. Pupils are accepted at the beginning of each semester. Entrance requirements are that the applicant must be (1) at least twenty years of age; (2) free from sickness or handicap which may prove to be a deterrent to effective teaching; (3) a graduate of the "grundskola" or equivalent with satisfactory grades in Swedish, English, history, civics, mathematics, physics, chemistry, and art, or shows that he has otherwise acquired the necessary knowledge; and (4) a graduate of a vocational course for cabinet makers and a vocational course for metal workers with at least three years in one course and one year in the other. Comparable work experience may be substituted. (12, pp. 1324-25).

Seventy-two students are normally accepted each fall semester, and an additional forty-eight are enrolled during the spring semester, as shown in Table I. Those who enroll during the spring semestter continue their schooling during the fall semester of the next school year. The majority of students are men, and a considerable number, as shown in Table I, are not admitted to the Institute.

Primary emphasis in instruction is placed on teacher education courses, as indicated in Table II. A few general education courses and mathematics and science are included while physical education is an elective subject.

In the course in sloyd methodology the students learn the fundamentals of teaching sloyd. Lesson preparation, choice of projects, development of courses of study, planning of sloyd rooms, and work in common materials are some of the subjects in the course. A great deal of time is devoted to work on

TABLE I

Students Applying and Admitted to the Sloyd Teachers Institute
Linkoping, Sweden (16, p. 3).

| Time | Number of Students | | Percentage |
	Applying	Admitted	Admitted
Fall 1960	424	48	11.3
Spring 1961	215	48	22.3
Fall 1961	346	72	20.8
Spring 1962	212	48	22.6
Fall 1962	288	72	25.0
Spring 1963	183	48	26.2
Fall 1963	268	72	26.9
Spring 1964	166	48	28.9
Fall 1964	274	72	26.3
Spring 1965	136	48	35.4
Fall 1965	231	72	31.2
Total	2,743	648	23.6

simple projects which are appropriate for students in the "grundskola." The problem of understanding the capacities of the child is rather great at the beginning for the average student in the Sloyd Teachers Institute since many are skilled craftsmen when they start their teacher education.

Psychology and pedagogy involve a basic understanding of psychology and its relation to teaching and to children. The history of sloyd and its role in education, and the teaching of practical and vocational subjects are studied.

Art consists of freehand sketching and the study of design principles, art and sloyd subjects. Only one and a half period per week is devoted to drawing since the students have had considerable experience in the field. Technical studies involve a study of materials, tools, and machines. (18, p. 3.)

Practical teaching experience is gained in schools in the area of Linkoping. One day a week is set aside for this purpose. A teacher from the Institute is coordinator of the program, while sloyd teachers in the public schools are responsible for the actual teaching experiences the future teachers receive.

A voluntary program of practical teaching experience is also part of the training of sloyd teachers. Under this program children of the community come to the Sloyd Teachers Institute one evening each week. They are taught by students under the supervision of a sloyd instructor. During the fall semester of 1965 there were sixty-eight students in eighteen groups with each group being taught by a student teacher. (17, pp. 19-22).

TABLE II

Course in the Sloyd Teachers Institute
Linkoping, Sweden (16, p. 4)

Course	Periods per week
Sloyd Methodology	10
Practice Teaching	6
Art	5.5
Psychology and Pedagogy	5
Swedish	2
Mathematics	2
Physics and Chemistry	2
Drawing	1.5
Civics	1
Technical Studies	1
Total Required Subjects	36
Physical Education, elective	2
Total	38

The Sloyd Teachers Institute has a director (rektor) and a faculty consisting of sloyd teachers, art and drawing teachers, and teachers of special subjects such as mathematics, physics, chemistry, civics, psychology, and physical education. The maximum teaching load for the director is six hours per week and twenty-three hours per week for teachers in sloyd methodology. Teachers of special subjects (adjunkt) teach a maximum of nineteen hours per week. (12, p. 1326).

Facilities and equipment of the Sloyd Teachers Institute are specifically designed to meet the needs of the students and the program. Hence, tools and machines are of the same type that are found in the sloyd programs in the "grundskola." Since skill development is not a goal of the instruction, machines are held to a minimum. Sloyd rooms for metal work, wood work, and crafts such as work in straw, leather, plastic, and paper are utilized in sloyd methodology. A library containing about 1,800 volumes is conveniently located and frequently used by the students. A special photo library containing more than 1,000 colored slides of interesting projects is available for study.

There is no tuition at the Sloyd Teachers Institute. Room and board as well materials required in the course work are paid by the students. Study loans and scholarships are available.

The future development of sloyd teacher education depends to some extent on the development of sloyd itself. The so-called "picture and form" type of sloyd which is being promoted by some educators would require a re-examination of the present system of educating sloyd teachers. Sloyd teachers and students have also expressed some concern about the present form of sloyd teacher education. In a survey of students at the Sloyd Teachers Institute in 1965 about 60 per cent of second semester students indicated that their experience at the vocational schools had been too long and production centered to be of much benefit for sloyd teachers. Sixty-four per cent of the students said that they had no use for skills they had acquired in the vocational school. Nearly 99 per cent of the students thought the course at the Sloyd Teachers Institute was too short and 100 per cent would like to attend the Institute an additional year. The majority of students suggested two years of practical vocational experience followed by three years of teacher preparation at the Sloyd Teachers Institute. (19, pp. 1-3).

A proposal submitted to the National Board of Education by Thorsten Lundberg, director of the Sloyd Teachers Institute, and Per Gartell, a sloyd teacher, suggests that the course for sloyd teachers be extended to three years. Entrance requirements would include the same general education requirements as for other teachers, but only one year of practical work experience or vocational school as compared to the present four years of vocational experience or education. (4, pp. 1-3).

Vocational Teachers

Vocational teachers instruct in a variety of subjects in local, regional, private, and corporation schools, as well as in the pre-vocational programs of "grundskola" and in retraining programs. There are four basic groups of teachers of vocational subjects; vocational teachers (teachers in trade and industrial areas), teachers of domestic science (home economics), teachers in nursing and related areas, and teachers of business and distributive education. (10, p. 269). Only the first group will be described.

The largest group of vocational teachers is in the metals area with other large groups teaching automechanics, painters, repairmen-blacksmiths-welders, and carpenters. (6, p. 1). There are more than fifty occupations in which vocational teachers instruct. 8, p. 25).

Vocational teachers in public institutions have, in general, received teacher training in addition to a rather lengthy period of practical training. Teachers in private and corporation schools have often attended special short courses in teaching metholodgy in addition to the practical work experiences. Many vocational teachers have earned an engineering degree.

In order to become a vocational teacher in a public institution a person must meet certain requirements set forth by law. The same general requirements as for the sloyd teacher with regard to health, ability to teach, and knowledge about subject matter must be met. In addition, the vocational teachers must have seven years of practical work experience in the field of specialization and must have graduated from a vocational-pedagogical institute. In order to receive a permanent appointment, the vocational teacher must have taught successfully for at least two years. (10, pp. 268-70).

Vocational teachers are required to teach thirty-six hours per week while the director or principal, depending on the size of the school, is required to teach from four to twenty hours each week. (10, pp. 267, 272).

Teachers in permanent positions in local vocational schools are appointed by the county education board upon the recommendation of the local school board. Administrative appointments are made by the National Board of Education upon the recommendation of local school boards and the approval of the county education board. Appointments for administrative positions are usually for a period of six years. (10, pp. 1155-1163).

Permanent teacher appointments at schools under the jurisdiction of the county are made by the board of each school. Administrative appointments at these schools are made by the National Board of Education.

Teachers and administrators of private and corporation schools which receive state aid are appointed by that school's board for an indefinite or definite period of time.

Evaluation of vocational teachers for the purpose of filling permanent positions in public institutions is based, as in the case of sloyd teachers, on a system of merits including teaching ability, knowledge and skills, and time spent as a teacher. In the category of teaching ability the vocational teacher is given points in the same manner as for the sloyd teacher. Five points are awarded for each year of related practical experience before becoming a teacher. Three additional points are added for each year in a vocational school and for passing the journeyman test. Credit is given attendance in technical institutes, an engineering degree, and grades in these schools. Special courses are awarded additional points.

The computation of nearly every teacher's credits must be based on pertinent regulations. (3, pp. 410-414, 465-466, 473-474). The point system for evaluation of credits for a vocational teacher with twelve years of teaching experience, seven years of practical work experience, and certain types of education is shown in Table III. The multiplier indicates that teaching skill shown during the student teaching period in the vocational-pedagogical institute carries most weight, while practical experience comes next.

Another group of teachers of vocational subjects are the lay or part-time teachers. These teachers do not need to meet specific requirements as to pedagogical training, but they must know their subject matter field. These teachers are utilized extensively in many vocational and technical schools, especially in part-time classes which meet in the evening. The combination technical-vocational school in Linkoping, Sweden, with a part-time enrollment of about 1,300 students employs more than 100 lay teachers representing nearly fifty different vocations. (16, pp. 16-30).

Vocational Teacher Education

Teachers of vocational subjects receive their professional or pedagogical training at six teacher training institutions referred to as vocational-pedagogical institutes (yrkespedagogiska institut). These institutes are organized by the National Board of Education in conjunction with existing vocational schools.

In addition to the course at the vocational pedagogical institutes, shorter courses in teaching methodology are also organized for teachers who have not received teacher training at a vocational-pedagogical institute. This is sometimes the case of older teachers and teachers in private and corporation schools. Specific subject matter courses of about fifteen weeks duration are organized when such a need exists. (13, p. 176).

Since 1960, all teachers must have attended the one-year course at one of the vocational-pedagogical institutes in order to qualify as a vocational teach-

TABLE III

Point System for Evaluation of Vocational Teacher Credits

Type of Credits	Points	Multi-plier	Total Number of Points
Pedagogic Institute, one year course	2.0	1.0	2.0
Grade, teaching skill	3.0	12.0	36.0
Grade, teaching aptitude	2.5	3.0	7.5
Grade, industriousness*	3.0	0.0	0.0
Practical Experience, seven years**	5.0	7.0	35.0
Vocational School, two years	3.0	2.0	6.0
Technician Course, average of grades	2.5	5.0	12.5
Refresher Courses (2), each twelve days	1.0	1.0	1.0
Teaching Experience, first ten years	10.0	2.0	20.0
eleventh year	1.0	1.8	1.8
twelvth year	1.0	1.7	1.7
Practical Experience' Maximum six years	6.0	.25	1.5
Total			125.0

*Six (6) points are deducted if grade in industriousness is lower than the highest possible.

**No points are awarded for practical experience beyond seven years.

er. The entrance requirements for attendance at the institutes are that the applicants:

1. Have reached the age of twenty-two.
2. Are free from sickness or handicap which may make a person unsuitable for teaching.
3. Have completed with satisfactory grades the seven-year "folkskola," or the "grundskola."
4. Have acquired all-around skill and knowledge in the vocation in which the applicants plan to become teachers through at least seven years of practical work experience. (13, pp. 177-178).

Because of the large number of applicants these minimum requirements are seldom sufficient for admission. Most students who are admitted have worked as foremen or engineers and have attended technical institutes, engineering schools, or otherwise improved their education. The number of applicants admitted to the six institutes varies somewhat, but it is a small fraction of the total number of applicants. At the Institute in Linkoping, for example, only 178 students were admitted of a total number of 1,302 eligible persons who sought admission to the school for the fall semester of 1964. (16, pp. 28-31) Similar admission rates are found in the other institutes.

Instruction in vocational-pedagogical institutes is based on a course of study prepared by the National Board of Education. The program is both of a general professional and a specific vocational nature. During the first period of fifteen weeks, lectures are given in study techniques, pedagogy, psychology, safety, and administration and organization of the schools as well as the labor market. Seminars and the workshops are held in teaching techniques, speech, and the use of audio-visual aids. Students are given an opportunity to present lectures and demonstrations both in general vocational areas and in their own specific field. Several visits to industries are made during this period. (23, p. 1-14).

The second fifteen week period is devoted to student teaching in various vocational schools and "grundskolor" in and around the community. During this time the student teachers are under the supervision of an approved master teacher in each of the schools.

The last three weeks of the school year are devoted to review of the more important facets of teacher education, reports of experiences during the student teaching period, and special projects and studies. In addition, a final examination is administered during this period.

Facilities and equipment of the vocational pedagogical institutes are primarily of class room character with the necessary equipment for related theoretical instruction. Practice demonstrations which may utilize shops and shop equipment are performed in the vocational school's facilities of which the institute is a part.

There are no fees or tuition for attending vocational-pedagogical institutes. Students are paid a salary somewhat lower than they will receive as teachers upon completion of the course, and they are also reimbursed for travel to and from the institute. (13, p. 178).

Teachers who attend short-term courses are paid the same salary as when teaching in addition to travel and living expenses while away from home. (9, 1).

The future development of vocational teacher education is likely to change somewhat with the introduction of the comprehensive "gymnasium" school (a comprehensive secondary school with academic, vocational, and technical branches) and the completed development of the nine-year "grundskola." The Commission which planned the proposed "gymnasium" school will, in the near future, investigate and make a proposal for the future form of vocational teacher education. The Commission has already established that the length of time involved in both the practical and the theoretical phases of preparing vocational teachers probably does not need to be equal for all vocations. Hence, it is likely that certain vocational teachers may not need to have seven years of practical work experience before they enroll in the vocational-pedagogical institute. (8, pp. 250-255). The National Board of Education has also proposed an increase in the number of teachers of vocational subjects. A seventh institute is likely to be established to meet this need for more vocational education teachers. (1, pp. 366-368).

Technical Education Teachers

Technical education teachers are employed in technical institutes, the technical line of the "gymnasium" and the technological line of the "fackskola" (a two-year secondary institution somewhat resembling the junior college). As the "fackskola" replaces the technical institutes nearly all technical education teachers will be employed in the "gymnasium" or "fackskola."

Teachers in the "fackskola" and the "gymnasium," in general, meet the same requirements as to education and experience. In fact, technical education teachers may teach in both types of schools.

Qualifications for permanent teaching posts in the technological line of the "fackskola" and the "gymnasium" are, at present, mainly a university degree in two or three subject matter areas such as physics and electronics, and a period of practical teacher training. The highest rank of teachers is the senior master (lektor) position which requires a licentiate degree and qualifications in teaching two or three subjects as well as a certain attainment in university studies. (Some "lektors" have the doctor's degree.) The other rank is assistant master (adjunkt); a permanent or a non-permanent position. In order to be appointed to a permanent position, however, the teacher must have taught for a minimum of two years and have met the other standard requirements of health, fitness, and education. (10, pp. 1117-1118). Part-time teachers are also employed in technical education programs.

Teachers are appointed to permanent positions by the county school board, except in the case of the position of "lektor" which is appointed by the National Board of Education upon the recommendation of the local school board.

An evaluation of a technical teacher's credits proceeds as in the evaluation of sloyd and vocational education teachers. More emphasis is placed on academic achievements such as degrees, courses, grades, matriculation examinations, and dissertations. For technical education teachers who have an engineering degree such subjects as drawing, design, construction and practical work experience are awarded credits. (3, pp. 418-430).

Salaries of teachers in technical schools or in technical subjects rank higher than salaries of vocational teachers, who, in turn rank somewhat higher than sloyd teachers. In general, elementary teachers receive lower salaries than teachers in secondary schools including vocational schools and "fackskolor."

Teachers in the technical areas of the "fackskola" are prepared in essentially two ways. They may have an engineering degree from a "gymnasium" or from a university and to this have added some practical teacher training; or they may have studied under a special program which prepares teachers in technical subjects.

For persons who have an engineering degree and plan to become teachers, the National Board of Education has organized practical teacher training courses in various institutions. Persons who take these courses are paid salaries as if they were teaching. For those who have a university degree the course is normally one semester long and consists of special theoretical pedagogical education and practical teaching experiences in a school under the guidance of a master teacher. The "gymnasium" trained engineer takes a full one-year course. The first semester is devoted entirely to supplementary mathematics, physics, and pedagogy. During the second semester the program consists of practical and theoretical teacher training as in the case of the university trained engineer. In order to enroll in the course a person must have an engineering degree, be at least twenty-two years of age, and have two years of work experience in the field. (13, pp. 180-184).

The second road to becoming a technical education teacher begins after successful completion of the "gymnasium" course. These prospective teachers seek admission to a three-year institution which prepares them to teach either technical physics and electricity-electronics, or technical physics and machine technology. There were three such schools accepting 125 students during the fall of 1965. Entrance requirements are primarily completion of "gymnasium" with good grades in the scientific and technical subjects. Practical work experience is desirable, but not necessary for admission. The course of study is three years followed by one semester of pedagogical training and another semester of practice teaching under the guidance of a master teacher. Hence, the length of schooling is actually four years, although only three years are spent at the institute. (5, pp. 94-95).

In the summer of 1965 the National Committee on Teacher Training recommended that teachers in "gymnasium" and "fackskola" have four years of education beyond the "gymnasium," and one year of practical and theoretical teacher education in order to become assistant masters. Senior masters would need six years of study at a university and an additional year of teacher training. An integration of teaching methodology and subject matter was, however, recommended instead of the strict separation of subject matter and teaching methodology which has been prevalent. Teachers of technical subjects would be Masters of Science and Masters of Technology. Because of the expansion of the secondary school system it is expected that about 2,000 teachers need to be trained in the technical field during the next few years. (2, pp. 96-99).

Various types of financial aid are available for students who wish to become teachers in "fackskola" or "gymnasium." Direct government grants of approximately 875 Swedish crowns (175 American dollars), and loans of up to 2,485 Swedish crowns (495 American dollars), are made available to the students for each semester. (14, p. 11).

Teacher Organizations

In few countries of the world has trade unionism reached such an advanced state of development as in Sweden. There are unions representing manual workers, white collar workers, and professional people. In fact, employers have established their own organization in order to better deal with labor problems.

Teachers have organized into associations which have both a professional purpose and the traditional union purpose of welfare of the individual. Most teachers of sloyd, vocational, and technical subjects are affiliated through their particular organizations with the Central Organization of Salaried Employers (Tjanstemannens Centralorganization). The Central Organization of Salaried Employers represented in 1963 thirty-three unions or associations having a total of 465,000 members. (22, pp. 12-13).

183

The Central Organization represents member organizations in matters of common concern when a collective approach is required. It negotiates in matters involving salaries and general conditions of employment.

Most sloyd, vocational, and technical teachers become members of the Central Organization of Salaried Employers through the Association of Handicrafts and Skilled Trades Teachers (Svenska Facklararforbundet). This Association is composed of twenty organizations representing teachers of vocational subjects, technical subjects, sloyd, music, art, textile, and special education. The total membership was about 14,250 in 1964. (1, pp. 96-97). The Central Organization has taken over much of the trade union type of activities of each of the member organizations. Some vocational organizations have thus been able to deal only with problems of a professional nature.

Sloyd teachers are organized into a national organization (Slojdlararnas Riksforening) with a membership of about 1,700 sloyd teachers. The purposes of the organization are to promote and guard the sloyd teachers' economical and social interests and to further the development of sloyd. (21, p. 266).

The Vocational Education Teachers Association (Yrkesutbildningens Lararforening) is composed of teachers of vocational subjects and has about 3,000 members. Technical education teachers with a membership of about 200 and vocational school principals with a membership of 350 have their own organizations. All of these organizations for sloyd, vocational and technical education teachers, and principals of vocational schools are affiliated with the Association of Handicrafts and Skilled Teachers. (1, pp. 96-98).

Teachers in "gymnasium" and "fackskola" who have a university degree may belong to the Association of Swedish Secondary School Teachers which has about 10,000 members. This Association is in turn affiliated with the Swedish Confederation of Professional Associations (Sveriges Akademikers Central-organisation). The Confederation has thirty member organizations representing professional people with university degrees. The total membership is about 50,000.

The Swedish Confederation of Professional Associations is both a professional association and a trade union and in this respect similar to other organizations of teachers and other professional people. It has participated in the planning of the school reforms in Sweden as well as in problems connected with university education. It has entered into collective bargaining with employers (state, local government, private) in order to improve conditions of the profession. Negotiations are carried on each year with government and local authorities concerning salaries and conditions of employment. Occasionally the Confederation has authorized blockades of certain teaching positions, meaning that qualified persons are advised not to apply for certain positions when they become vacant. A kind of strike has also been called a few times by arranging for a certain number of employees to hand in their resignations. Although the majority of disputes have been resolved without direct action, the Confederation states that "it is always necessary to be well prepared for strike action, for, in the last analysis, it is the danger of a labor dispute that makes an employer disposed to make concessions." (20, p. 23). During the fall semester of 1966 a strike was called which lasted for several weeks, and although schools were not closed (students took over teaching duties) the dispute with the State was both involved and intense. Some interesting events took place, in addition to the students acting as teachers. Mrs. Erlander, the Prime Minister's wife was among the striking teachers while her husband tried first to avert the strike and after the strike, to settle it.

In the vocational field there is the Swedish Vocational School Organization (Svenska yrkesskolforeningen), a wholly professional organization. The members of this organization consist of (1) private and public schools of vocational nature, industry and business concerns, and vocational interest groups, and (2) teachers, administrators, and board members at vocational schools as well as individual persons interested in promoting and developing vocational education. The purpose of the Swedish Vocational School Organization is to promote sound development of vocational education, higher standards among vocational schools, better cooperation between schools, state, and various occupational interest groups, and better and continuing preparation of vocational teachers. (1, pp. 93-96).

SUMMARY

Teacher education in Sweden has not kept pace with the developments in elementary, secondary, and vocational education. The future will probably see changes in the education of both sloyd and vocational teachers. The prestige and good salaries and the advantageous financial arrangements for eduction of sloyd, vocational, and technical teachers has made recruiting of teachers a problem of selection rather than of promotion.

FOOTNOTE REFERENCES

1. Bergstrom, Erik (ed.), *Yrkesutbildningens handbok*. Borlange, Sweden, Svenska yrkesskolforeningen, 1965.
2. Dahllof, Urban, Sven Zetterlund, and Henning Oberg, *Gymnasiet och fackskolan*. Stockholm, Sweden, Svenska Bokforlaget, 1965.
3. Frankman, Frenne, "Meritvardering vid tillsattning av vissa larartjanster, Skoloverstyrelsens anvisningar 24 februari 1959 jamte tillagg och andringar," *Skollagen och skolstadgan*. Lund, Sweden, Hakan Ohlssons forlag, 1964.
4. Gartell, Per, and Thorsten Lundberg, "Till Kungl. Skoloverstyrelsen, Forslag till forandrad slojdlararutbildning," April, 1964, (Mimeographed.)
5. Kungliga Arbetsmarknadsstyrelsen, *Student 66*. Stockholm, Sweden, Kungliga Arbetsmarknadsstyrelsen, 1965.
6. ——————. "Yrkeslarare/industri- och hantverksyrken," *Yrkesupplysningar*. Stockholm, Sweden, Arbetsmarknadsstyrelsen, 1964.
7. Kungliga Ecklesiastikdepartementet, *Lararutbildningen*. Statens offentliga utredningar 1965:29, Stockholm, Sweden, Kungliga Ecklesiastikdepartementet, 1965.
8. ——————. Yrkesutbildningsberedningen, *Yrkesutbildningen*. Statens offentliga utredningar 1966:3, Lund, Sweden, Hakan Ohlssons forlag, 1966.
9. Kungl. Maj:ts, *Oavkortad lon till larare vid yrkesskolor m.m.* Kungligt brev 26.2.1965.
10. ——————. *Skolstadga*. Svensk forfattningssamling 439, 1962.
11. ——————. *Stadga for ovningslarare*. (Ovingslararstdaga), Svensk forfattningssamling 507, 1960.
12. ——————. *Stadga for slojdlararseminariet*. Svensk forfattningssamling 511, 1960.

13. Kungliga Skoloverstyrelsen, "Bestammelser angaende lararutbildningskurser for ingenjorer," *Aktuellt fran Skoloverstyrelsen.* 18:180-184, 1964/65.
14. _____. *Lararyrket ger mer framtid.* Stockholm, Sweden, Skoloverstyrelsen, 1964.
15. *Ljungstedtska Skolan.* Linkoping, Sweden, AB Ostgotatryck, 1965.
16. Ljungstedtska Skolan, *Redogorelse for arbetsaret 1964-1965*, Linkoping, Sweden, Ljungstedtska skolan, 1965.
17. Slojdlararseminariet, *Katalog HT-65*. Linkoping, Sweden, Slojdlararseminariet i Linkoping, 1965.
18. _____. *Redogorelse for lasaret 1964-1965.* Linkoping, Sweden, Slojdlararseminariet, 1965.
19. _____. "Sammanfattning av enkat bland slojdlararseminariets elever angaende slojdlararutbildningen," Linkoping, Sweden, Slojdlararseminariet, 1965, (Mimeographed).
20. Sveriges Akademikers Centralorganisation, *Swedish Professional Associations as Trade Unions.* Stockholm, Sweden, Svergies Akademikers Centralorganisation, 1959.
21. Sveriges lararforbund, *Arsbok for skolan.* Stockholm, Sweden, Sveriges lararforbund, 1964.
22. Tjanstemannens Centralorganisation. *This is TCO.* Stockholm, Sweden, Brolins/ab vi technar och trycker, n.d.
23. Yrkespedagogiska institutet, Stockholm, "Skoloverstyrelsens Kurs nr 730418, Forelasningar m.m. vid pedagogisk kurs for yrkeslarare och blirande yrkeslarare, anordnad i Stockholm under tiden 10 januari—29 april 1966," Stockholm, Sweden, Yrkspedagogiska institutet, n. d. (Mimeographed.).

AUTHOR INDEX

KEY-WORD TITLE INDEX